Level D
Contents

BASIC Phonics Skills

Basic Phonics Skills
What's in Level D?

Reproducible Skill Sheets

Choose from a number of reproducibles to practice each skill.
Skill sheets present varying levels of difficulty to meet individual student needs.

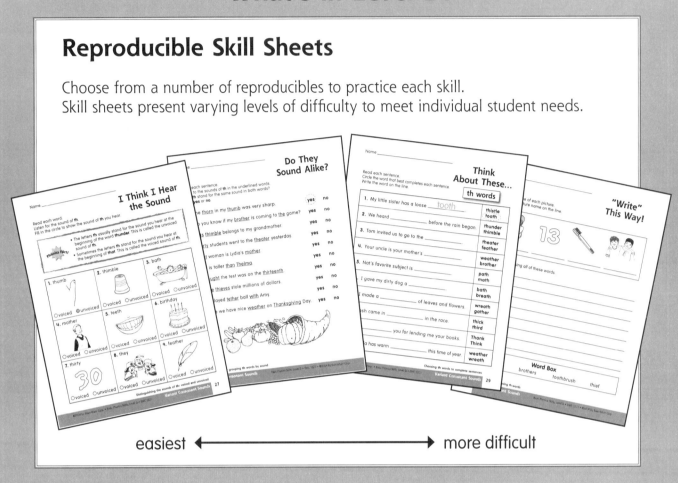

easiest ←————————————→ more difficult

Review provided in each skill section.

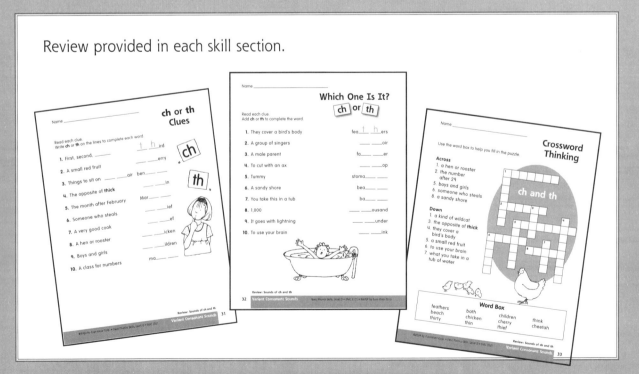

Word Family Practice Sheets

Word Family reading lists provide repeat practice of major word families.

Activity sheets reinforce word families presented on the reading lists.

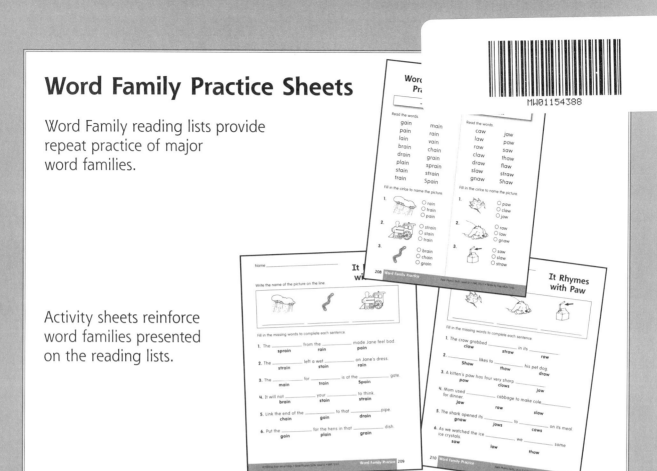

20 Little Phonics Readers

Materials

- story forms, reproduced for each student
- scissors
- stapler

Steps to Follow

1. Copy a book for each student.
2. Cut out the pages on the dotted lines.
3. Fold the pages on the solid lines.
4. Place pages 2, 3, 4, and 5 inside the front cover section.
5. Fit the book into the stapler and staple in the outside spine.

Tracking Student Progress

Use the form on page 5 to record the progress of each student. The rubric below will help you assess each student's level of competence. Students who fail to achieve a 2 or 3 level should be provided with additional instruction and practice until they become proficient.

Mastered **3**	• The student is able to complete the activity independently. • The student is able to complete the activity correctly. • The student is able to answer questions about the phonetic principle being practiced.
Showed Adequate Understanding **2**	• The student is able to complete the activity with little assistance. • The student is able to complete the activity with minimal errors. • The student is able to answer some questions about the phonetic principle being practiced.
Showed Inconsistent Understanding **1**	• The student required assistance to complete the activity. • The student made several errors. • The student did not appear to understand the phonetic principle being practiced.
Showed Little or No Understanding **0**	• The student required one-to-one assistance to complete the activity, or was unable to complete the activity. • The student made many errors. • The student showed no understanding of the phonetic principle being practiced.

Basic Phonics Skills, Level D
Student Record Form

Name _____

Sound or Skill Practiced	Level D Page Number	Date Completed	3 Mastered	2 Showed Adequate Understanding	1 Showed Inconsistent Understanding	0 Showed Little or No Understanding

Basic Phonics Skills, Level D • EMC 3321 • ©2004 by Evan-Moor Corp.

The Benefits of Phonics Instruction

Words are made of letters, and letters stand for sounds. That is the simple basis for providing phonics instruction to all beginning readers. Research has shown that all children will benefit from being taught the sound-spelling connection of the English language (Chall, 1967). Phonics instruction leads to decoding, which gives beginning readers one more strategy to use when faced with an unfamiliar word.

Research has shown the following to be true:

- Strong decoding skills in early readers correlate highly with future success in reading comprehension (Beck and Juel, 1995).

- As more and more "sounded-out" words become sight words, readers have more time to devote to the real reason for reading: making meaning from print (LaBerge and Samuels, 1974; Freedman and Calfee, 1984).

- Readers who are good decoders read more words than those who are poor decoders (Juel, 1988).

- Children with limited learning opportunities and abilities benefit most from phonics instruction, but more able children also benefit (Chall, 1967).

- Those who are successful decoders do not depend on context clues as much as those who are poor decoders (Gough and Juel, 1991).

The best readers can decode words. As a result, those readers grow in word recognition, fluency, automaticity, and comprehension. "Sounding out" unfamiliar words is a skill that benefits all readers. These new words quickly become "sight words," those recognized immediately in text, which allow the reader to spend more time on new words. This cycle is the foundation that creates reading success, and successful readers are better learners.

Basic Phonics Skills, Level D • EMC 3321 • ©2004 by Evan-Moor Corp.

Variant Consonant Sounds

Name _____

The Sounds of c

- When the letter **c** is followed by the vowels **a**, **o**, or **u** (and most consonants), it usually stands for the /k/ sound, as in **cat**.
- When the letter **c** is followed by the vowels **e**, **i**, or **y**, it usually stands for the /s/ sound, as in **city**.
- After one short vowel, the /k/ sound is spelled **ck**.

Read the word.
Listen for the sound of **c**.
Circle the sound you hear: /k/ or /s/.

1. duck — (/k/) /s/	**2.** ceiling — /k/ /s/	**3.** can — /k/ /s/
4. cup — /k/ /s/	**5.** bucket — /k/ /s/	**6.** princess — /k/ /s/
7. celery — /k/ /s/	**8.** candy — /k/ /s/	**9.** corn — /k/ /s/

Distinguishing the sounds of c: /k/, /s/

Name _____

Which Sound of c?

Look at the words in the word box.
Listen for the sound of **c** in each word.
Do you hear /k/ or /s/?
Write each word in the correct box.

 **c**at

 **c**ircus

/k/

castle

/s/

Word Box

race	princess	candle	castle	pencil
catnip	fancy	icy	decide	curb
cereal	because	uncle	pecan	celery

Matching or grouping **c** words by sound

Name _____

Read and Think

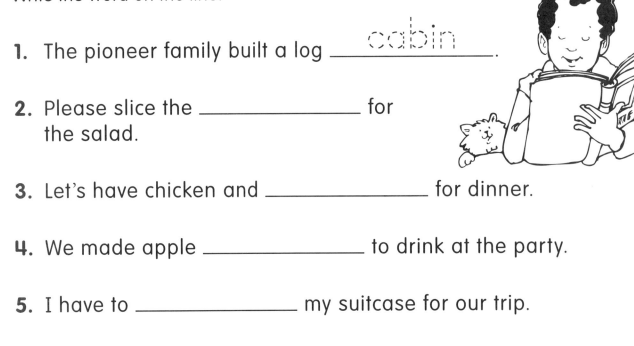

Read each sentence.
Choose the word from the word box that
best completes each sentence.
Write the word on the line.

1. The pioneer family built a log __cabin__.

2. Please slice the _____ for
   the salad.

3. Let's have chicken and _____ for dinner.

4. We made apple _____ to drink at the party.

5. I have to _____ my suitcase for our trip.

6. Amy spread chocolate frosting on the _____.

7. Yuki learned to fasten the _____ on her shoe.

8. I ate a big _____ of juicy watermelon.

Word Box

slice	cabin	cider	cupcakes
pack	cucumber	rice	buckle

Choosing **c** words to complete sentences

Name _____

Read each pair of words.
Write one sentence using both words.

1.	space	captain
2.	iceberg	canoe
3.	computer	voice
4.	juicy	cube
5.	truck	race

Writing sentences using **c** words

Name _____

By George, It's a g!

Phonics Fact!

- When the letter **g** is followed by the vowels **a**, **o**, or **u**, it usually stands for the /g/ sound, as in **goat**.
- When the letter **g** is followed by the vowels **e** or **y**, it usually stands for the /j/ sound, as in **gem**.

Read the word.
Listen for the sound of **g**.
Circle the sound you hear: /g/ or /j/.

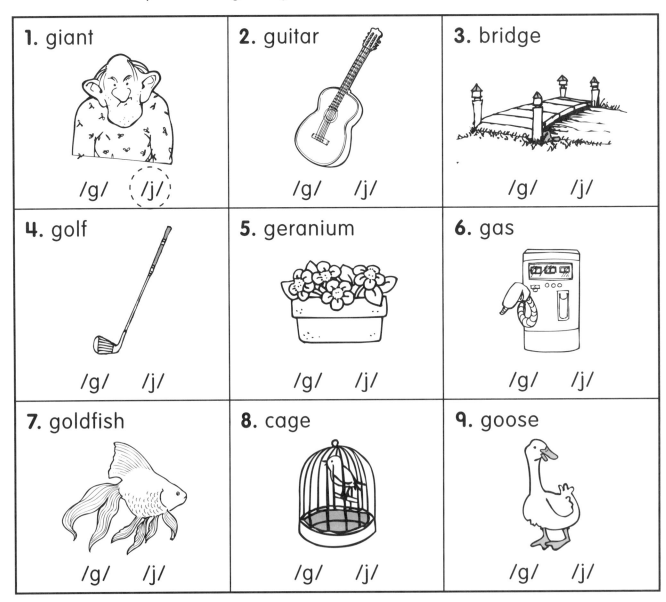

1. giant /g/ (/j/)	**2.** guitar /g/ /j/	**3.** bridge /g/ /j/
4. golf /g/ /j/	**5.** geranium /g/ /j/	**6.** gas /g/ /j/
7. goldfish /g/ /j/	**8.** cage /g/ /j/	**9.** goose /g/ /j/

Distinguishing the sounds of g: /g/ and /j/

 Basic Phonics Skills, Level D • EMC 3321 • ©2004 by Evan-Moor Corp.

Name _____

Look at the words in the word box.
Listen for the sound of **g** in each word.
Write each word in the correct box.

 **G**eorge

/j/

giraffe

 **G**abe

/g/

Word Box

tiger	giraffe	sugar	flag	huge
sponge	frog	ginger	page	gym
gum	gem	wagon	gave	

Matching or grouping **g** words by sound

Name _____

Missing Words

Read each sentence and the word choices.
Circle the word that best completes
each sentence.
Write the word on the line.

/j/ or /g/

1. Firefighters face ~~danger~~ every day.	(**danger**) **dragons**
2. Tony _____ when his dad makes funny faces.	**gathers** **giggles**
3. Marsha used an old _____ to wash her car.	**cage** **rag**
4. The prospector found a huge _____ of pure gold.	**nugget** **vegetable**
5. The towel I left out in the rain is all _____.	**soggy** **guilty**
6. The plants on the window _____ get plenty of sun.	**log** **ledge**
7. The _____ told us all about the bears in the park.	**ranger** **hunger**
8. Mom put some oil on the squeaky _____.	**finger** **hinge**
9. An _____ is a large lizard that lives in the tropics.	**iguana** **judge**
10. I put the lawnmower in the _____.	**gift** **garage**

Choosing **g** words to complete sentences

14 **Variant Consonant Sounds** Basic Phonics Skills, Level D • EMC 3321 • ©2004 by Evan-Moor Corp.

Name _____

Read each pair of **g** words.
Write one sentence using both words.

1.		fudge	Gary
2.		pigeon	gate
3.		signal	change
4.		igloo	strange
5.		gym	game

Writing sentences using **g** words

Name _____

The Sounds of s

- The letter **s** usually stands for the /s/ sound, as in **sun**.
- Sometimes the letter **s** stands for the /sh/ sound, as in **sure**.
- Sometimes the letter **s** stands for the /z/ sound, as in **music**.
- Sometimes the letter **s** stands for the /zh/ sound, as in **treasure**.

Read the word. Listen for the sound of **s**.

Circle the sound the letter **s** stands for in the words.

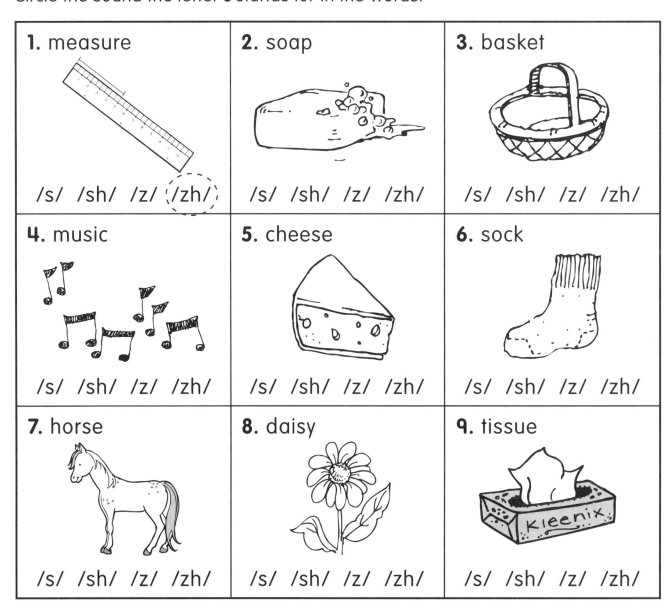

1. measure	**2.** soap	**3.** basket
/s/ /sh/ /z/ (/zh/)	/s/ /sh/ /z/ /zh/	/s/ /sh/ /z/ /zh/
4. music	**5.** cheese	**6.** sock
/s/ /sh/ /z/ /zh/	/s/ /sh/ /z/ /zh/	/s/ /sh/ /z/ /zh/
7. horse	**8.** daisy	**9.** tissue
/s/ /sh/ /z/ /zh/	/s/ /sh/ /z/ /zh/	/s/ /sh/ /z/ /zh/

Distinguishing the sounds of s: /s/ /sh/ /z/ /zh/

Name _____

The Sun Sure Is Not Easy to Measure

Read each word in the word box.
Listen for the sound of the letter **s**.
Write each word in the correct box.

/s/ as in **sun**	/sh/ as in **sure**
sink	

/z/ as in **easy**	/zh/ as in **measure**

Word Box

sink	wise	sure	tissue
miss	measure	easy	raisin
sugar	glass	treasure	pleasure

Matching or grouping **s** words by sound

Name _____

Missing Words

Read each sentence.
Circle the word that best completes
each sentence.
Write the word on the line.

1. A _____raisin_____ is a dried grape.	(raisin) easy
2. You use a _____ to wipe your nose.	easy tissue
3. A bone that has turned to stone is called a _____.	fossil glass
4. In pirate stories, the _____ is always found in a trunk.	measure treasure
5. We say _____ when we ask someone to help us.	please raisin
6. A _____ is a person who takes care of sick people.	sure nurse
7. Someone who knows a lot is _____.	wise easy
8. Something that can't be seen is _____.	tissue invisible

Choosing **s** words to complete sentences

Name _____

The Musician

Read each sentence.
Choose the word that best completes the sentence.
Write the word on the line.

1. Alvin likes ___music___ lessons.

2. He always puts his flute back in

the _____.

3. He plays best in the _____ of C and F.

4. Alvin got a dozen _____ at his last performance.

5. He was _____ to get them.

6. Alvin's dad works at the _____ where lots of old
instruments are displayed.

7. He thinks it is a _____ to play the flute.

8. One day, Alvin may be a _____ musician.

Word Box			
famous	pleasure	surprised	case
keys	roses	music	museum

Choosing **s** words to complete sentences

Name _____

Say the name of each picture.
Find the word in the word box.
Label each picture by writing the word on the line.

mouse _____   _____   _____   _____

Write a story using all of these words.

_____

_____

_____

_____

_____

_____

_____

Word Box			
sugar	treasure	mouse	cheese

Writing sentences using **s** words

Name _____

Solve the Clues

Read each clue.
Write **c**, **g**, or **s** on the line or lines to
complete each word.

1. A penny   _____ent

2. A dog's tail does this   wa_____

3. Frozen water   i_____e

4. A jewel   _____em

5. Something sweet to chew   _____um

6. You use it to smell   no_____e

7. Fuel for a car   _____a_____

8. More than one mouse   mi_____e

9. Part of a book   pa_____e

10. Food made from milk   chee_____e

11. A running contest   ra_____e

12. Something to drink from   _____up

13. A pet bird lives in it   _____a_____e

14. Something you play   _____ame

"**c**"
"**g**"
"**s**"

Review: Sounds of **c**, **g**, and **s**

Name _____

Which Word?

Write the word that names each picture.
Then answer the questions.

1.  frog _____	**2.**  _____	**3.**  _____
4. 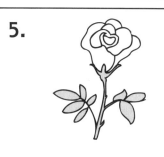 _____	**5.**  _____	**6.**  _____

7. Which word contains the /j/ sound of the letter **g**? _____

8. Which word contains the /s/ sound of the letter **c**? _____

9. Which word contains the /z/ sound of the letter **s**? _____

10. Which word contains the /sh/ sound of the letter **s**? _____

Word Box

giant	corn	giraffe	tissue	pencil
frog	rose	hose	city	wagon

Review: Sounds of **c**, **g**, and **s**

22 **Variant Consonant Sounds**   Basic Phonics Skills, Level D • EMC 3321 • ©2004 by Evan-Moor Corp.

Name _____

Choose the Sounds of ch

Phonics Fact!

- The letters **ch** usually stand for the /ch/ sound you hear at the beginning of the word **cherry**.
- Sometimes the letters **ch** stand for the /sh/ sound you hear at the beginning of the word **chef**.
- Sometimes the letters **ch** stand for the /k/ sound you hear at the end of the word **stomach**.

Read the word.
Listen for the sound of **ch**.
Circle the sound you hear: /ch/, /sh/, or /k/.

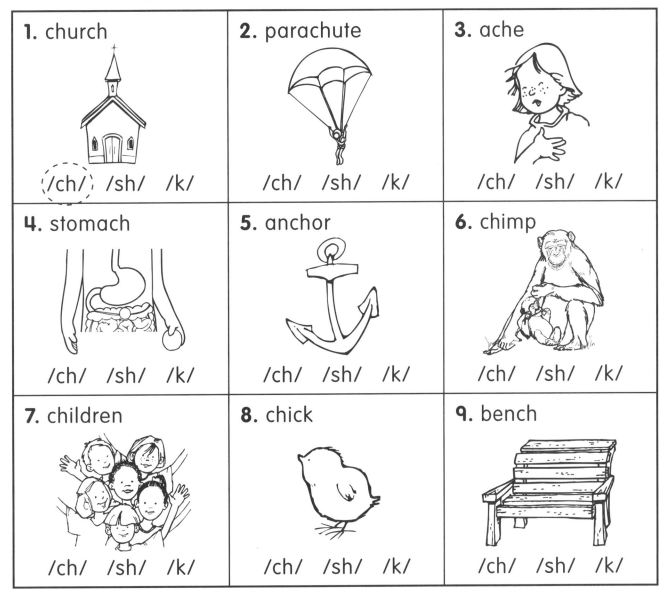

1. church
/ch/ /sh/ /k/

2. parachute
/ch/ /sh/ /k/

3. ache
/ch/ /sh/ /k/

4. stomach
/ch/ /sh/ /k/

5. anchor
/ch/ /sh/ /k/

6. chimp
/ch/ /sh/ /k/

7. children
/ch/ /sh/ /k/

8. chick
/ch/ /sh/ /k/

9. bench
/ch/ /sh/ /k/

Distinguishing the sounds of **ch**: /ch/ /sh/ /k/

Name _____

Underline the **ch** in each word.
Listen to the sound **ch** makes.
Write each word in the correct box.

chick

para**ch**ute

tootha**ch**e

/ch/	/sh/	/k/
church		

Word Box

church	chemical	cheetah	chute
chiffon	peach	chest	stomach
ranch	change	chowder	chapter

Matching or grouping ch words by sound

Basic Phonics Skills, Level D • EMC 3321 • ©2004 by Evan-Moor Corp.

Name _____

Riddle It

Read each riddle.
Choose the **ch** word from the box that solves the riddle.
Use a complete sentence to write the answer.

1. I am a tasty fruit.

I am a peach.

2. I help you float to the ground.

_____

3. I am an animal that can run very fast.

_____

4. Smoke comes out of me.

_____

5. I am used to keep a boat in place.

_____

6. I am a small limb of a tree.

_____

7. I am another name for a cook.

_____

8. I am used to make work easier.

_____

Word Box			
chimney	pèach	anchor	machine
parachute	chef	cheetah	branch

Choosing **ch** words to complete sentences

Name _____

I Can Write Sentences

Read each pair of words.
Write one sentence using both words.

1.		children	couch
		_____	
		_____	
2.		chef	kitchen
		_____	
		_____	
3.		chips	crunch
		_____	
		_____	
4.		pinch	stomach
		_____	
		_____	
5.		orchard	peaches
		_____	
		_____	

Writing sentences using **ch** words

Variant Consonant Sounds   Basic Phonics Skills, Level D • EMC 3321 • ©2004 by Evan-Moor Corp.

Name _____

Read each word.
Listen for the sound of **th**.
Fill in the circle to show the sound of **th** you hear.

I Think I Hear the Sound

Phonics Fact!

- The letters **th** usually stand for the sound you hear at the beginning of the word **thunder**. This is called the unvoiced sound of **th**.

- Sometimes the letters **th** stand for the sound you hear at the beginning of **that**. This is called the voiced sound of **th**.

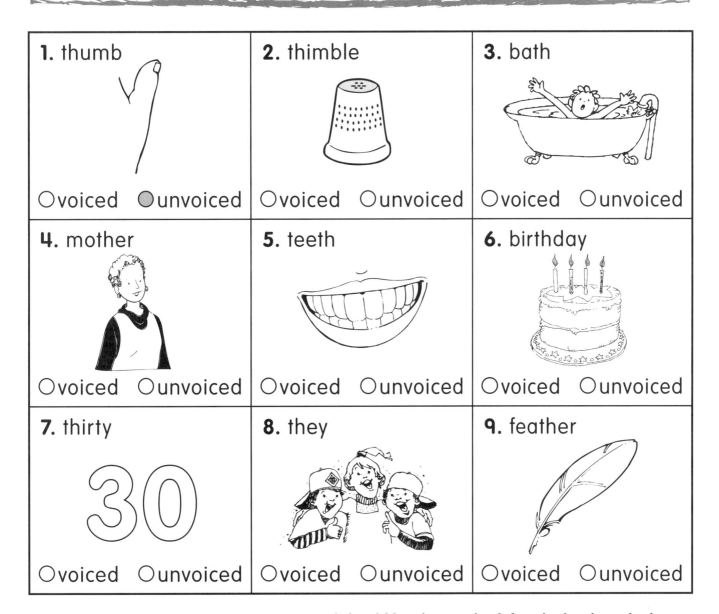

1. thumb
○voiced ●unvoiced

2. thimble
○voiced ○unvoiced

3. bath
○voiced ○unvoiced

4. mother
○voiced ○unvoiced

5. teeth
○voiced ○unvoiced

6. birthday
○voiced ○unvoiced

7. thirty
○voiced ○unvoiced

8. they
○voiced ○unvoiced

9. feather
○voiced ○unvoiced

Distinguishing the sounds of **th**: voiced and unvoiced

Name _____

Do They Sound Alike?

Read each sentence.
Listen to the sounds of **th** in the underlined words.
Does **th** stand for the same sound in both words?
Circle **yes** or **no**.

1. The <u>thorn</u> in my <u>thumb</u> was very sharp.   (yes)   no

2. Do you know if my <u>brother</u> is coming to <u>the</u> game?   yes   no

3. <u>This</u> <u>thimble</u> belongs to my grandmother.   yes   no

4. <u>Thirty</u> students went to the <u>theater</u> yesterday.   yes   no

5. <u>That</u> woman is Lydia's <u>mother</u>.   yes   no

6. Rick is taller <u>than</u> <u>Thelma</u>.   yes   no

7. I <u>thought</u> the test was on the <u>thirteenth</u>.   yes   no

8. <u>Those</u> <u>thieves</u> stole millions of dollars.   yes   no

9. Lee played <u>tether</u> ball <u>with</u> Amy.   yes   no

10. I hope we have nice <u>weather</u> on <u>Thanksgiving</u> Day.   yes   no

Matching or grouping **th** words by sound

Basic Phonics Skills, Level D • EMC 3321 • ©2004 by Evan-Moor Corp.

Name _____

Think About These...

Read each sentence.
Circle the word that best completes each sentence.
Write the word on the line.

th words

1. My little sister has a loose _____tooth_____.	thistle ⟨tooth⟩
2. We heard _____ before the rain began.	thunder thimble
3. Tom invited us to go to the _____.	theater feather
4. Your uncle is your mother's _____.	weather brother
5. Nat's favorite subject is _____.	path math
6. I gave my dirty dog a _____.	bath breath
7. I made a _____ of leaves and flowers.	wreath gather
8. Josh came in _____ in the race.	thick third
9. _____ you for lending me your books.	Thank Think
10. Florida has warm _____ this time of year.	weather wreath

Choosing **th** words to complete sentences

Name _____

"Write" This Way!

Say the name of each picture.
Write the picture name on the line.

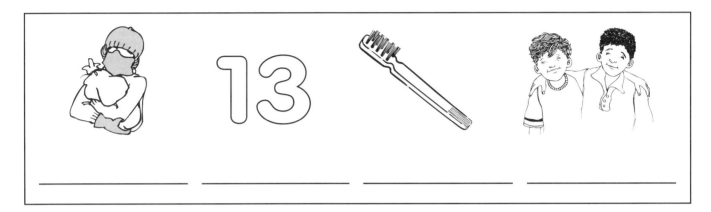

_____ _____ _____ _____

Write a story using all of these words.

_____

_____

_____

_____

_____

_____

_____

Word Box

thirteen   brothers   toothbrush   thief

Writing sentences using th words

Name _____

Read each clue.
Write **ch** or **th** on the lines to complete each word.

1. First, second, _____   __t__ __h__ird

2. A small red fruit   ____ ____erry

3. Things to sit on   ____ ____air   ben____ ____

4. The opposite of **thick**   ____ ____in

5. The month after February   Mar____ ____

6. Someone who steals   ____ ____ief

7. A very good cook   ____ ____ef

8. A hen or rooster   ____ ____icken

9. Boys and girls   ____ ____ildren

10. A class for numbers   ma____ ____

Review: Sounds of ch and th

Name _____

Which One Is It?

Read each clue.
Add **ch** or **th** to complete the word.

1. They cover a bird's body   fea___ ___ers

2. A group of singers   ___ ___oir

3. A male parent   fa___ ___er

4. To cut with an ax   ___ ___op

5. Tummy   stoma___ ___

6. A sandy shore   bea___ ___

7. You take this in a tub   ba___ ___

8. 1,000   ___ ___ousand

9. It goes with lightning   ___ ___under

10. To use your brain   ___ ___ink

Review: Sounds of ch and th

Name _____

Crossword Thinking

Use the word box to help you fill in the puzzle.

Across

1. a hen or rooster
2. the number after 29
5. boys and girls
6. someone who steals
8. a sandy shore

Down

1. a kind of wildcat
3. the opposite of **thick**
4. they cover a bird's body
5. a small red fruit
6. to use your brain
7. what you take in a tub of water

ch and th

Word Box

feathers	bath	children	think
beach	chicken	cherry	cheetah
thirty	thin	thief	

Review: Sounds of **ch** and **th**

©2004 by Evan-Moor Corp. • Basic Phonics Skills, Level D • EMC 3321   **Variant Consonant Sounds** 33

Name _____

Attention!

Read each word.
Underline the **ti**, **si**, or **ci**.
Then circle **yes** or **no** to answer the question.

1. decoration  Do you hear /sh/? **yes** **no**	**2.** lotion  Do you hear /sh/? **yes** **no**	**3.** ticket  Do you hear /sh/? **yes** **no**
4. delicious  Do you hear /sh/? **yes** **no**	**5.** musician  Do you hear /sh/? **yes** **no**	**6.** signal Do you hear /sh/? **yes** **no**
7. nation  Do you hear /sh/? **yes** **no**	**8.** mission  Do you hear /sh/? **yes** **no**	**9.** cinnamon roll  Do you hear /sh/? **yes** **no**

Recognizing words with the /sh/ sound spelled ti, si, and ci

Name _____

Fill in the Blanks

Choose the correct ending for each word.
Write the letters on the lines.

-tion	-cial

1. lo____ t i o n

6. frac____ ____ ____ ____

2. na____ ____ ____ ____

7. subtrac____ ____ ____ ____

3. so____ ____ ____ ____

8. addi____ ____ ____ ____

4. ac____ ____ ____ ____

9. sta____ ____ ____ ____

5. po____ ____ ____

10. spe____ ____ ____ ____

What do you call a country full of autos?

A car-na____ ____ ____ ____

Using chunks to write **ti** and **ci** words

Name _____

Sentence Completion

Read each sentence.
Choose the word that best completes
each sentence.
Write the word on the line.

1. A train is one kind of ___transportation___.

2. I need _____ from my house to yours.

3. A large mass of ice is called a _____.

4. Something that tastes good is _____.

5. A picture in a book is called an _____.

6. Put _____ on your dry skin.

7. Our _____ is the USA.

8. A _____ is a number for a part of the whole.

Word Box

directions	delicious	nation	transportation
illustration	glacier	lotion	fraction

Choosing ti and ci words to complete sentences

Basic Phonics Skills, Level D • EMC 3321 • ©2004 by Evan-Moor Corp.

Name _____

Read each pair of words.
Write a sentence using both words.

1.		delicious	potion
		_____	
		_____	
2.	Invitation	decoration	invitation
		_____	
		_____	
3.		vacation	action
		_____	
		_____	
4.	$23 + 8 = 31$ $31 - 8 = 23$	addition	subtraction
		_____	
		_____	
5.		musician	motion
		_____	
		_____	

Writing sentences with **ti**, **si**, and **ci** words

Silent Letters

Name _____

Silent b

Sometimes a letter in a word makes no sound.
It is called a **silent letter**.

crum~~b~~

Read each word.
Circle the silent **b**.
Which word does <u>not</u> have a silent **b**?
Cross it out.

| 1. lamb | 2. climb | 3. comb |
| 4. limb | 5. thumb | 6. club |

Write the missing word on the line.

1. The _____ nibbled on the grass.

2. Will you _____ your hair?

3. Let me _____ up the ladder.

Identifying the silent **b** appearing in a word

Name _____

Fill in the silent **b** in each word.
Read the word.
Match the word to its picture.

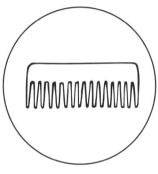

1. crum___

2. lam___

3. thum___

4. lim___

5. com___

6. clim___

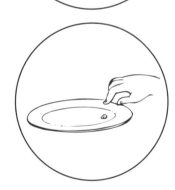

Write the words that complete the sentence.

Tom likes to _____ out on the

_____ of the oak tree.

numb   **limb**   **climb**

Name _____

Reading Words with Silent b

Read each sentence.
Fill in the circle by the word that
best completes each sentence.
Write the word on the line.

comb

1. Pam packed a brush and a _____.
   ● **comb**   ○ **climb**

2. The little _____ cried for its mother.
   ○ **limb**   ○ **lamb**

3. Pick up the _____ on the rug.
   ○ **crumb**   ○ **thumb**

4. I pinched my _____ in the back door.
   ○ **crumb**   ○ **thumb**

5. Let's trim the large _____ of that tree.
   ○ **lamb**   ○ **limb**

6. Please _____ up and get me that cup.
   ○ **limb**   ○ **climb**

Cross out the silent letters.
Circle the words that do <u>not</u> have silent letters.

bulb	climb	rubber	limb
lamp	branch	thumb	plumber

Completing sentences with silent **b**

Name _____

Silent h

Phonics Fact!

Sometimes a letter in a word makes no sound.
It is called a **silent letter**.

r~~h~~yme

Read each word.
Circle the silent **h**.
Which word does <u>not</u> have a silent **h**?
Cross it out.

1. honest	**2.** rhino	**3.** cheetah
4. hour	**5.** ghost	**6.** hand

Write the missing word on the line.

1. The alarm clock rang every _____.

2. I saw the _____ at the zoo climb the tree.

3. The _____ cried, "Ooo!"

Identifying the silent h appearing in a word

Basic Phonics Skills, Level D • EMC 3321 • ©2004 by Evan-Moor Corp.

Name _____

Fill in the silent **h** in each word.
Read the word.
Match the word to its picture.

1. rino

2. cheeta_____

3. _____our

4. r_____ubarb

5. g_____ost

6. _____onest

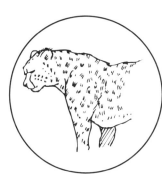

Write the words that complete the sentence.

Mom made a _____ pie one

_____ before dinner.

hour   **honest**   **rhubarb**

Name _____

Invisible h

Read each word in the word box.
Trace over the silent **h** in the words.

Word Box

| cheetah | rhubarb | rhinoceros | rhyme |
| ghost | honest | herb | hour |

Choose the word that best answers the question.
Write the word on the line.

1. Which is a measurement of time? _____ hour _____

2. Which is an animal that runs very fast? _____

3. Which means "truthful"? _____

4. Which lives in a haunted house? _____

5. Which means words whose end sounds
   are alike? _____

6. Which is a tart-tasting stalk that can
   be made into a pie? _____

7. Which is a large animal with a horn? _____

8. Which is a plant that seasons food? _____

Name _____

Silent n

Phonics Fact! Sometimes a letter in a word makes no sound.
It is called a **silent letter**.

autumn

Read each word.
Circle the silent **n**.
Which words do <u>not</u> have a silent **n**?
Cross them out.

1.	2.	3.
autumn	seven	column
4.	5.	6.
pencil	hymn	man

Write the missing word on the line.

1. The leaves begin to fall in the _____.

2. We sang a _____ at church.

3. I tied the dog leash around the _____.

Identifying the silent n appearing in a word

Name _____

Autumn Time

Read each sentence.
Choose the word that best completes
each sentence.
Write the word on the line.

1. Rico enjoys raking the leaves every _autumn_.

2. Terry packed a brush and a _____
   in her bag.

3. It is always best to be _____.

4. Josh got a rose thorn stuck in his _____.

5. I like to read long poems that _____ and
   tell a story.

6. The mother sheep followed her _____ around the
   meadow.

7. The scouts learned to _____ a small mountain.

8. Toshi hung a swing from the _____ of
   the maple tree.

Word Box

thumb	autumn	comb	rhyme
limb	lamb	climb	honest

Review: Completing sentences with silent b, n, and h words

Basic Phonics Skills, Level D • EMC 3321 • ©2004 by Evan-Moor Corp.

Name _____

Silent g

Sometimes a letter in a word makes no sound.
It is called a **silent letter**.

g̷narl

Read each word.
Circle the silent **g**.
Which word does <u>not</u> have a silent **g**?
Cross it out.

1.	2.	3.
g̷haw	gnome	gift
4.	5.	6.
sign	gnat	gnu

Write the missing word on the line.

1. My dog loves to _____ on a juicy bone.

2. We put a For Sale _____ on our house
   last night.

3. The _____ flicked his tail at the pesky fly.

Identifying the silent **g** appearing in a word

Name _____

Silent k

 **Phonics Fact!**

Sometimes a letter in a word makes no sound.
It is called a **silent letter**.

~~K~~nit

Read each word.
Circle the silent **k**.
Which word does <u>not</u> have a silent **k**?
Cross it out.

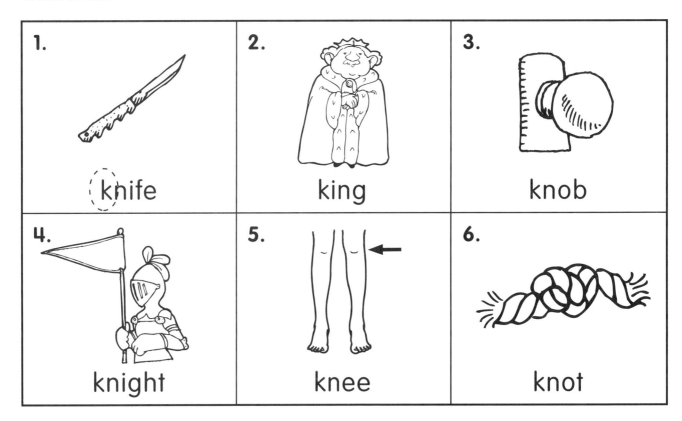

1. knife	**2.** king	**3.** knob
4. knight	**5.** knee	**6.** knot

Write the missing word on the line.

1. Tie a _____ in the rope to hold it.

2. Turn the _____ to open the door.

3. Use the sharp _____ carefully.

Identifying the silent **k** appearing in a word

48 **Silent Letters**   Basic Phonics Skills, Level D • EMC 3321 • ©2004 by Evan-Moor Corp.

Name _____

Kneel, Gnome!

Read the word. Circle the silent letter.
Draw a line to match the word to its picture.

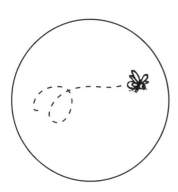

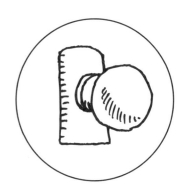

1. knife

2. gnome

3. knit

4. gnat

5. knock

6. knot

7. knee

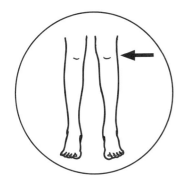

8. knob

Reading words with a silent k or g

Name _____

Do You Know?

Read each sentence.
Choose the word that best completes the sentence.
Write the word on the line.

1. Our class is learning to _____knit_____ hats out of yarn.

knob	knit

2. The _____ is a funny-looking animal.

gnu	gnaw

3. "Be careful with that sharp _____," said Gran.

knuckle	knife

4. Tim loves to read about the _____ of the Round Table.

knives	knights

5. The puppy _____ on everything in sight.

gnaws	gnats

6. We had to go inside because the _____ were flying all around us.

gnus	gnats

Completing sentences with silent **k** and **g** words

Name _____

Grumpy Old Gnome

Phonics Fact!

Sometimes the letter pairs **gn** or **kn** stand for the /n/ sound.
The letters **g** and **k** are silent.

g̸nat   K̸not

Read the poem.
Find nine words in the poem that have a silent **g** or **k**.
Underline each word.
Draw an **X** on the silent letter **g** or **k**.

A grumpy old g̸nome
In his dark little home,
Stared at his knuckles
And gnawed on a bone.

He had gnarly fingers,
And gnats in his hair.
Gnashing his teeth,
He exclaimed, "I don't care!"

"Don't knock on my door.
Don't kneel by my throne.
I'm a grumpy old gnome.
Just leave me alone!"

Review: Choosing words with silent k and g: kn-, gn-

Name _____

Silent c

Sometimes the letter pair **sc** stands for the /s/ sound.
The letter **c** is **silent**.

sċenery

Read each word.
Circle the silent **c**.
Which word does <u>not</u> have a silent **c**?
Cross it out.

| 1. scent | 2. scientist | 3. camp |
| 4. scissors | 5. muscles | 6. scepter |

Write the missing word on the line.

1. You will have to use your _____ to pick up that big box.

2. Use your orange _____ to cut out the shapes.

3. The king carried his _____ in the parade.

Identifying the silent **c** appearing in a word

Name _____

This Makes Scents!

Phonics Fact!

Sometimes the letter pair **sc** stands for the /s/ sound.
The letter **c** is silent, as in **scissors**.

Read each sentence.
Choose the word that best completes the sentence.
The correct word will have a silent **c**.

1. The _____scenery_____ along the coast of California is beautiful.

scrape	scenery

2. The _____ of warm gingerbread filled the house.

scent	cent

3. Lian likes to study _____ because she wants to learn about nature.

scary	science

4. Mr. Ahmad used a pair of _____ to cut the fabric.

schools	scissors

5. The weightlifter wants to build strong _____.

biscuits	muscles

6. The queen held her jeweled _____.

scepter	scream

Choosing words with silent c

Name _____

Silent c
Match-up

Fill in the silent **c** in each word.
Read the word.
Match the word to its picture.

1. s__issors

2. mus__les

3. s__epter

4. s__ent

5. s__enery

Write the word that completes the sentence.

I hurt my leg _____ during the race at school.
        scissors   **muscles**

Reading words with silent c

Basic Phonics Skills, Level D • EMC 3321 • ©2004 by Evan-Moor Corp.

Name _____

Silent w

Sometimes the letter pair **wr** stands for the /r/ sound.
The **w** is **silent**.

ẃreck

Read each word.
Circle the silent **w**.
Which word does <u>not</u> have a silent **w**?
Cross it out.

1. wren	**2.** wagon	**3.** wrench
4. wrist	**5.** wreath	**6.** wrote

Write the missing word on the line.

1. Use the big _____ to fix the broken pipe.

2. I _____ my story late last night.

3. Did you hang a _____ on your front door?

Identifying the silent **w** appearing in a word

Name _____

Fill in the silent **w** in each word.
Read the word.
Match the word to its picture.

1. __w__rist

2. ____rite

3. ____reck

4. ____reath

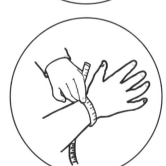

5. ____ren

6. ____rench

Write the words that complete the sentence.

The little _____ made her nest in the

_____ hanging on the front door.

wrench   **wreath**   **wren**

Reading words with silent w

Basic Phonics Skills, Level D • EMC 3321 • ©2004 by Evan-Moor Corp.

Name _____

A Wrinkled Candy Wrapper

Read each sentence.
Fill in the circle by the word that best completes the sentence.
Write the word on the line.

1. Russ had an old candy ___wrapper___.
   - ○ **wreck**　　● **wrapper**

2. It had lots of _____.
   - ○ **wrinkles**　　○ **wrist**

3. Something was _____.
   - ○ **wren**　　○ **wrong**

4. Someone _____ on that wrapper.
   - ○ **wrote**　　○ **wrench**

5. He wrote about a car _____.
   - ○ **write**　　○ **wreck**

6. A man sprained his _____ in the wreck.
   - ○ **wren**　　○ **wrist**

7. They had to _____ his wrist.
   - ○ **wrote**　　○ **wrap**

8. It was hard to _____ on the wrapper.
   - ○ **write**　　○ **wrong**

9. The _____ was hard to read.
   - ○ **wrong**　　○ **writing**

Choosing words that begin with silent w to complete sentences

Name _____

Write the Right One

Read each sentence.
Fill in the circle by the word that best completes
each sentence.
Write the word on the line.

1. Mom used a __wrench__ to tighten the pipe.
   ● **wrench**   ○ **wreck**

2. The little brown _____ built a nest in the tree.
   ○ **whose**   ○ **wren**

3. Dr. Guzman _____ a bandage around Jim's arm.
   ○ **wrestled**   ○ **wrapped**

4. Vina _____ a letter to her grandmother.
   ○ **wrote**   ○ **wrist**

5. Jose pressed the _____ out of his pants.
   ○ **wrinkles**   ○ **whole**

6. Do you know _____ was sitting in this chair?
   ○ **who**   ○ **write**

7. The earthworm _____ in my hand.
   ○ **whoever**   ○ **wriggled**

8. It is _____ to steal from others.
   ○ **wrong**   ○ **wring**

9. Tamara memorized the _____ poem.
   ○ **whole**   ○ **whom**

10. Rosa made a _____ of flowers.
   ○ **wreath**   ○ **wrist**

Writing words with silent **w**

   Basic Phonics Skills, Level D • EMC 3321 • ©2004 by Evan-Moor Corp.

Name _____

Silent d

Read each word.
Circle the silent **d**.
Which word does <u>not</u> have a silent **d**?
Cross it out.

1. fudge

2. bridge

3. judge

4. glad

5. badge

6. hedge

Write the missing word on the line.

1. I love _____ with nuts in it.

2. Dad trimmed the _____ next to the house.

3. We drive over a _____ on the way to school.

Identifying the silent **d** appearing in a word

Name _____

Fill in the silent **d** in each word.
Read the word.
Match the word to its picture.

1. fu__d__ge

2. ba____ge

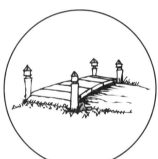

3. ju____ge

4. bri____ge

5. he____ge

6. we____ge

Write the words that complete the sentence.

The police officer wore a _____ as he

directed traffic across the _____.

bridge   **fudge**   **badge**

Reading words with silent d

Basic Phonics Skills, Level D • EMC 3321 • ©2004 by Evan-Moor Corp.

Name _____

Look for Silent d

Read each riddle.
Answer each riddle using a word that contains a silent **d**.
Write the word on the line.

1. I rule over a courtroom.
Who am I?   _____

2. I am a kind of candy.
What am I?   _____

3. A police officer wears me on her
uniform. What am I?   _____

4. I am a sort of fence made of bushes.
What am I?   _____

5. I am made to help people cross over
a river. What am I?   _____

6. I am a gentle push.
What am I?   _____

7. I am a short furry animal. I dig in
the ground. What am I?   _____

8. You can push me under a door to hold
it open. What am I?   _____

Word Box

fudge	wedge	judge	nudge
bridge	badge	hedge	badger

Choosing words with a silent **d**

Name _____

Silent l

Sometimes a letter in a word makes no sound.
It is a **silent letter**.

ta/k

Read each word.
Circle the silent **l**.
Which word does <u>not</u> have a silent **l**?
Cross it out.

| 1. half | 2. yolk | 3. wall |
| 4. calf | 5. salmon | 6. chalk |

Write the missing word on the line.

1. The baby _____ looked for its mother in the barn.

2. The teacher had _____ dust on her coat when she got home.

3. My sister loves to _____ on the phone.

Identifying the silent **l** appearing in a word

Name _____

Silent I
Match-up
Silent l
Match-up

Fill in the silent **l** in each word.
Read the word.
Match the word to its picture.

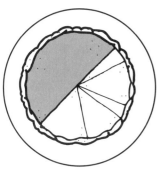

1. cha____k

2. wa____k

3. ta____k

4. ca____f

5. ha____f

6. sa____mon

Write the words that complete the sentence.

The _____ swam _____ way
up the river to the quiet pond.
half   **salmon**   **walk**

Reading words with silent l

©2004 by Evan-Moor Corp. • Basic Phonics Skills, Level D • EMC 3321   **Silent Letters**   **63**

Could You?

Read each sentence.
Choose the word that best completes each sentence.
Write the word on the line.

1. The _____yolk_____ is the yellow part of an egg.

2. We used _____ to draw pictures on the driveway.

3. We like to _____ about the books we are reading.

4. My brother went to Alaska to fish for _____.

5. The newborn _____ stood beside the mother cow.

6. Billy ate _____ of the large pizza.

7. Celery grows in _____.

8. The children like to _____ to school in the spring.

Word Box

half	chalk	calf	salmon
stalks	talk	yolk	walk

Choosing words with silent l

Name _____

Silent t

Sometimes a letter in a word makes no sound.
It is a **silent letter**.

fas̸ten

Read each word.
Circle the silent **t**.
Which word does <u>not</u> have a silent **t**?
Cross it out.

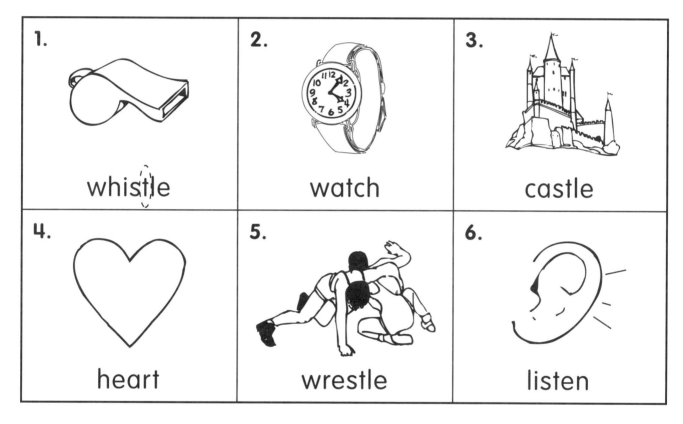

1. whistle	**2.** watch	**3.** castle
4. heart	**5.** wrestle	**6.** listen

Write the missing word on the line.

1. Don't blow that _____ in the house!

2. It is important to _____ closely in class.

3. The king rode his horse through the huge gate of the

_____ .

Identifying the silent **t** appearing in a word

Name _____

Fill in the silent **t** in each word.
Read the word.
Match the word to its picture.

1. wres____le

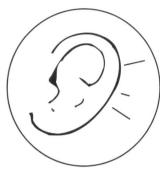

2. wa____ch

3. cas____le

4. lis____en

5. fas____en

6. whis____le

Write the words that complete the sentence.

Please _____ for the phone while you

_____ TV.

watch   **listen**   **fasten**

Reading words with silent t

Basic Phonics Skills, Level D • EMC 3321 • ©2004 by Evan-Moor Corp.

Name _____

Watch for Silent t

Read each sentence.
Fill in the circle by the word that best completes each sentence.
Write the word on the line.

1. Mandy left the butter out to _____soften_____.
   ○ **often**   ● **soften**

2. The pilot told us to _____ our seatbelts.
   ○ **fasten**   ○ **wrestle**

3. The referee blew his _____.
   ○ **latch**   ○ **whistle**

4. Chan used a _____ to chop some wood.
   ○ **hatchet**   ○ **hustle**

5. We made a big _____ of cookies.
   ○ **match**   ○ **batch**

6. The knights rode out of the _____ gate.
   ○ **castle**   ○ **nestle**

7. Our dog can _____ a ball in his mouth.
   ○ **stitch**   ○ **catch**

8. I always try to _____ carefully to directions.
   ○ **listen**   ○ **castle**

Writing words with silent t

Name _____

Silent gh

Sometimes letters in a word make no sound.
They are **silent letters**.

high

Read each word.
Circle the silent **gh**.
Which word does <u>not</u> have a silent **gh**?
Cross it out.

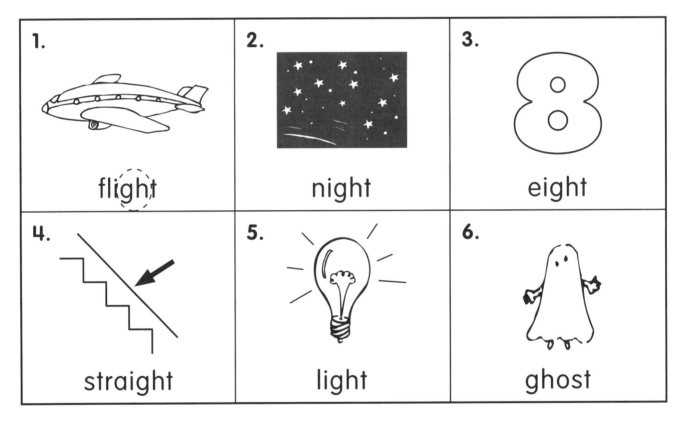

1. flight	**2.** night	**3.** eight
4. straight	**5.** light	**6.** ghost

Write the missing word on the line.

1. Draw a _____ line.

2. I would like _____ cookies, please.

3. The _____ sky was full of stars.

Identifying the silent **gh** appearing in a word

Name _____

Fill in the silent **gh** in each word.
Read the word.
Match the word to its picture.

1. ei__g__ __h__t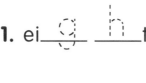

2. ni____ ____t

3. hi____ ____

4. fli____ ____t

5. strai____ ____t

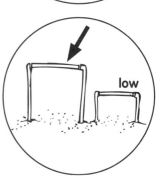

low

6. li____ ____t

Write the word that completes the sentence.

Do you sleep with a _____ on in your room?

light   **flight**   **night**

Name _____

Like Day and Night

Choose the word that best completes the sentence.
Write the word on the line.

1. The opposite of **low** is _____.

2. The opposite of **crooked** is _____.

3. The opposite of **dark** is _____.

4. The opposite of **loose** is _____.

5. The opposite of **left** is _____.

6. The opposite of **day** is _____.

Word Box
night   high   tight   light   right   straight

Name _____

Pick the Right One

Read each sentence.
Fill in the circle by the word that best completes
each sentence.
Write the word on the line.

1. Use the scale to see how much the baby __weighs__.
   ● **weighs**   ○ **sighs**

2. We always _____ to music on the radio.
   ○ **fasten**   ○ **listen**

3. A baby whale is called a _____.
   ○ **yolk**   ○ **calf**

4. Our parents do not like for us to _____.
   ○ **fight**   ○ **light**

5. Mary has _____ hair, but mine is very curly.
   ○ **height**   ○ **straight**

6. My grandparents take a _____ around the lake
   each morning.
   ○ **chalk**   ○ **walk**

7. How _____ do you brush your teeth?
   ○ **soften**   ○ **often**

8. I _____ never go swimming without a buddy.
   ○ **would**   ○ **half**

9. Dan's favorite jeans have _____ on them.
   ○ **patches**   ○ **latches**

Completing sentences with silent **l**, **t**, and **gh** words

Name _____

A Frightening Time

Choose the word that completes each sentence.
Write the word on the line.
Circle the silent letter or letters in each word.

1. Dad will ___fasten___ the carrier to the top of the van.

2. He fixed the _____ so the carrier would not slide around.

3. My sister's stuff took up _____ of the backseat.

4. Mom and Dad _____ about how much fun this vacation would be.

5. At the campsite, Dad cooked some fresh _____ on the grill.

6. The smoke drifted _____ above the trees.

7. Then we saw something scary that gave us a _____.

8. A huge black bear _____ toward our campsite!

Word Box			
fright	walked	salmon	high
fasten	latch	half	talked

Completing sentences with silent **l**, **t**, and **gh** words

Basic Phonics Skills, Level D • EMC 3321 • ©2004 by Evan-Moor Corp.

Name ___________________________________

Review Silent Letters

b, h, n, k

Read each word in the word box.
Cross out the silent letter.
Write each word in the correct box.

silent **b**	silent **h**
lamb	

silent **n**	silent **k**

Word Box

lamb	ghost	column	thumb
rhino	knife	comb	cheetah
hymn	knee	autumn	knot

Review: Silent letters

Name _____

Read each word in the word box.
Cross out the silent letter.
Write each word in the correct box.

silent **g**	silent **d**
sign	

silent **c**	silent **w**

Word Box

wrote	fudge	scissors	scent
sign	wrist	gnaw	wrench
muscle	gnome	gnat	judge

Review: Silent letters

Basic Phonics Skills, Level D • EMC 3321 • ©2004 by Evan-Moor Corp.

Name ______________________________

Review Silent Letters

t, l, b, gh

Read each word in the word box.
Cross out the silent letter or letters.
Write each word in the correct box.

silent **t**	silent **l**
listen	

silent **b**	silent **gh**

Word Box

yolk	talk	castle	wrestle
listen	flight	high	climb
light	comb	lamb	calf

Review: Silent letters

Search for Silent Letters

Read each word.
If you find a silent letter, circle it.
If there is no silent letter, cross out the word.

1.	comb	2.	hour
3.	rhino	4.	autumn
5.	thumb	6.	crumb
7.	column	8.	cheetah
9.	ghost	10.	candy
11.	honest	12.	paper

Review: Silent letters

Search for Silent Letters

Read each word.
If you find a silent letter, circle it.
If there is no silent letter, cross out the word.

1. (k)nob	2. gnaw
3. bread	4. knock
5. knot	6. sign
7. knife	8. knee
9. bug	10. scissors
11. muscles	12. craft

Review: Silent letters

Name _____

Search for
Silent Letters

Read each word.
If you find a silent letter, circle it.
If there is no silent letter, cross out the word.

1. 	wren	2. 	plant
3. 	fudge	4. 	write
5. 	half	6. 	happy
7. 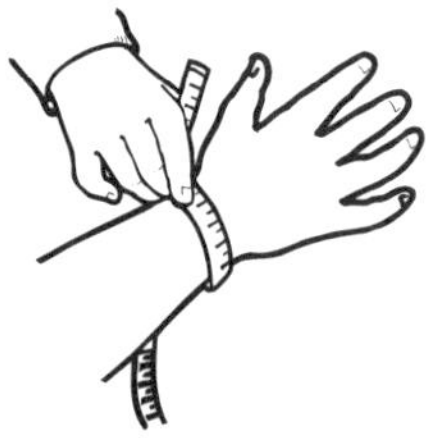	wrist	8. 	bridge
9. 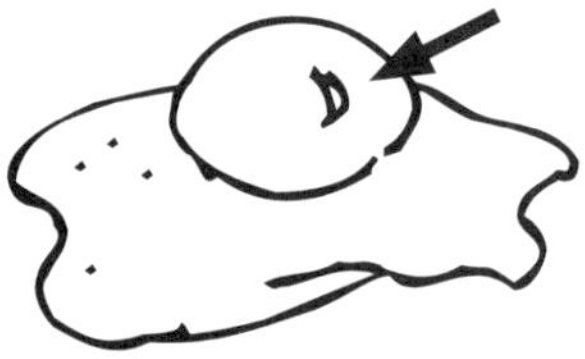	yolk	10. 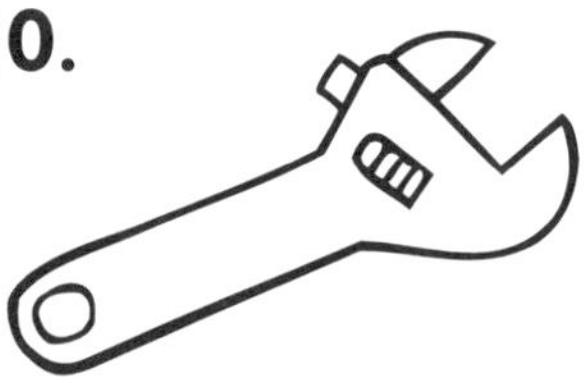	wrench
11. 	judge	12. 	calf

Review: Silent letters

Basic Phonics Skills, Level D • EMC 3321 • ©2004 by Evan-Moor Corp.

Name _____

Read each word.
If you find a silent letter, circle it.
If there is no silent letter, cross out the word.

1. whistle	2. watch
3. wagon	4. night
5. ghost	6. listen
7. eight	8. high
9. right	10. run
11. knee	12. knot

Name _____

Think and Write

Read each pair of words. Circle the silent letters.
Use both words in one sentence.

1.		lamb	climb
		_____	
		_____	
2.		thumb	rhino
		_____	
		_____	
3.		autumn	hour
		_____	
		_____	
4.		ghost	crumb
		_____	
		_____	
5.		gnome	gnaw
		_____	
		_____	

Writing sentences and strengthening awareness of silent letters

 Silent Letters   Basic Phonics Skills, Level D • EMC 3321 • ©2004 by Evan-Moor Corp.

Digraphs
Vowel and Consonant Digraphs

BASIC Phonics Skills

Name _____

Riddles

In some words, the letters **ai** or **ay** stand for the long **a** sound.

r<u>ai</u>n   **tr<u>ay</u>**

Choose the word that solves each riddle.
Write it on the line. Circle the vowel pair that
stands for the long **a** sound.

1. A dog wags me. What am I?   t<u>ai</u>l

2. Water runs down me. What am I?   _____

3. You use me to catch a fish. What am I?   _____

4. I catch the wind and help some boats go.
What am I?   _____

5. I am ice that falls from the sky. What am I?   _____

6. I am a mixture of black and white. What am I?   _____

7. You hit me with a hammer. What am I?   _____

8. You carry things on me. What am I?   _____

Word Box			
tail	hail	drain	sail
bait	gray	tray	nail

Long a digraphs: Writing words with **ai** or **ay**

Digraphs
Vowel Digraphs   Basic Phonics Skills, Level D • EMC 3321 • ©2004 by Evan-Moor Corp.

Name _____

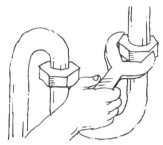

ai or ay?

Fill in the circle by the word that best completes
each sentence.
Write it on the line.
Circle the vowel pair that stands for the
long **a** sound.

1. Ray _____paid_____ to play an arcade game.
  ○ **maid**   ● **paid**   ○ **way**

2. We fed the chickens some _____.
  ○ **train**   ○ **gray**   ○ **grain**

3. Nat walked down the _____ to the river.
  ○ **trail**   ○ **rain**   ○ **train**

4. The hungry baby started to _____.
  ○ **ray**   ○ **raid**   ○ **wail**

5. Jerry used a _____ to repair the shelf.
  ○ **stray**   ○ **raid**   ○ **nail**

6. We filled the _____ pail with seashells.
  ○ **pain**   ○ **gray**   ○ **pay**

7. The plumber fixed the clogged _____.
  ○ **main**   ○ **wait**   ○ **drain**

8. I want to _____ this letter to my cousin.
  ○ **stay**   ○ **mail**   ○ **bail**

Long a digraphs: Completing sentences with **ai** and **ay** words

Name _____

They Take a Break

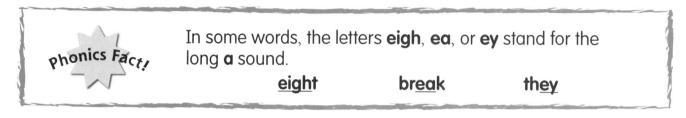

In some words, the letters **eigh**, **ea**, or **ey** stand for the long **a** sound.

eight   br**ea**k   th**ey**

Underline the vowel combination in each word that says /ā/.
Draw a line from each word to the picture it names.

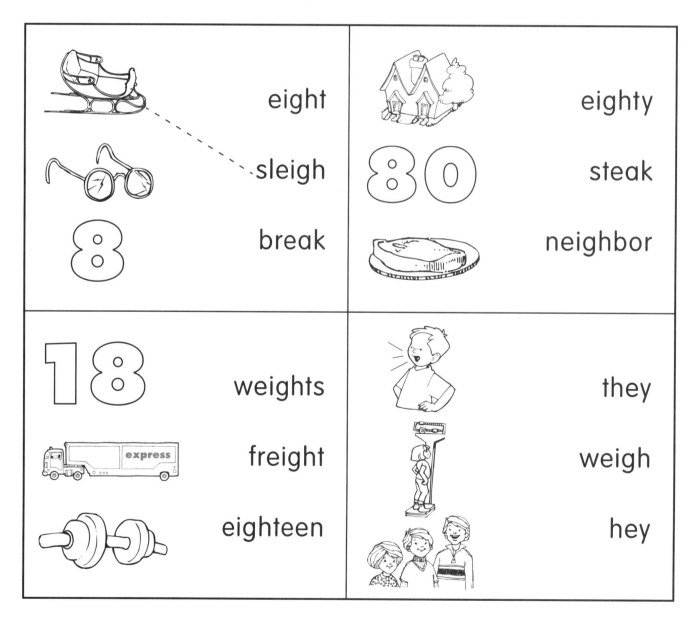

eight

sleigh

break

eighty

steak

neighbor

weights

freight

eighteen

they

weigh

hey

Long a digraphs: Choosing words with **eigh**, **ea**, or **ey**

Basic Phonics Skills, Level D • EMC 3321 • ©2004 by Evan-Moor Corp.

Name _____

What Says a?

Circle the letters in each word that
stand for the long **a** sound.

(eigh)t	eighty	break	neigh	prey
sleigh	great	neighbor	eighteen	whey

Read each clue.
Write the best answer or answers using words from the box.

1. Three words that tell how many   _____eight_____

_____

_____

2. To smash or split into parts   _____

3. A person who lives next to you   _____

4. A vehicle that can travel on snow   _____

5. An animal that is hunted for food   _____

6. The sound a horse makes   _____

7. Little Miss Muffet ate it with her curds   _____

8. Describes something very good
or very large   _____

Long a digraphs: Writing words with **eigh**, **ea**, or **ey**

Name _____

A Great Sale Today!

Read each sentence.
Choose the word that best completes
each sentence.
Write the word on the line.

1. On Saturday, my mom and I had a _____great_____ time.

2. We left around _____ o'clock in the morning.

3. It was garage sale day in our _____.

4. At the first place, I found an old Santa with his _____.

5. It was very fragile, so I had to be careful not to _____ it.

6. Mom found a set of _____ knives for a dollar.

7. She also found some _____ that looked brand new.

8. After shopping, I went home with only _____ cents!

Word Box			
neighborhood	eight	steak	sleigh
weights	great	break	eighty

Long **a** digraphs: Completing sentences with **ea** and **eigh** words

Basic Phonics Skills, Level D • EMC 3321 • ©2004 by Evan-Moor Corp.

Name _____

Read each pair of long **a** words.
Write a sentence using both words.

1.		train	away
2.		away	sleigh
3.		neighbor	mail
4.		gray	stain
5.		steak	they

Long a digraphs: Writing sentences with ai, ay, eigh, ea, or ey words

Name _____

Brain Buster

ai ay eigh words

Read each clue.
Write the word to complete the crossword puzzle.

Across

3. the opposite of **succeed**
4. something to sit on
6. frightened
8. an ache
9. 18
12. the month after April
13. 80
14. the opposite of **night**
15. people who break the
   law are sent to _____

Down

1. gave money to pay
   what you owe
2. to take part in a game
5. water that falls from
   the sky
7. to lift up
10. a color made when
    black and white are
    mixed
11. used with a hammer
12. letters sent and
    received

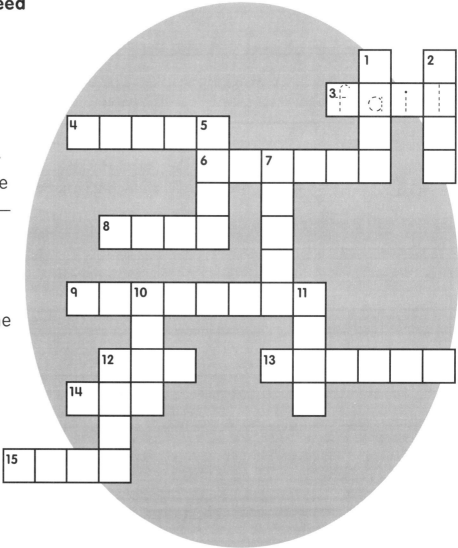

Word Box

afraid	eighteen	gray	nail	play	raise
chair	eighty	jail	May	pain	
day	fail	mail	paid	rain	

Review: Long a digraphs

88 Digraphs
Vowel Digraphs

Basic Phonics Skills, Level D • EMC 3321 • ©2004 by Evan-Moor Corp.

Name _____

What's Missing?

Write the missing letters to help
Elaine spell each word.

1. rtg	g	r	e	a	t
2. bt			a	i	
3. lh			a	i	
4. tl			a	i	
5. pr				a	y
6. nrg			a	i	
7. mn			a	i	
8. aw				a	y
9. tpn		a	i		

What vowel sound do you hear in all the words?

short **a**   long **a**   long **i**

Review: Long **a** digraphs

Name _____

Meet Long e Digraphs

In most words, the letter pairs **ea** and **ee** stand for the long **e** sound.

s<u>ea</u>   **tr<u>ee</u>**

Circle the letters in each word that say /ē/.
Draw a line from the word to the picture it names.

1. pea

2. team

3. bee

4. bead

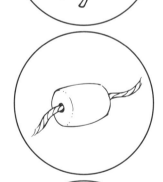

5. seal

6. leaf

7. beet

8. tree

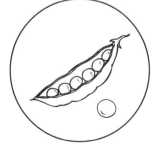

Long **e** digraphs: Choosing words with **ea** or **ee**

Digraphs
Vowel Digraphs

Basic Phonics Skills, Level D • EMC 3321 • ©2004 by Evan-Moor Corp.

Name _____

Read These Riddles

Read the words in the box.
Underline the letters that spell the long **e** sound.
Then write a word from the box to answer each riddle.

Word Box				
peak	beaver	clean	beep	green
feast	geese	weep	eagle	knead

1. I am the opposite of **dirty**. What am I? _____

2. I am something you do when you are sad. What am I? _____

3. I am a large meal. What am I? _____

4. I am a symbol of the United States. What am I? _____

5. I am the color of grass. What am I? _____

6. I am the sound made by a car horn. What am I? _____

7. I am an animal that builds dams. What am I? _____

8. I am something you do to bread dough. What am I? _____

9. Our babies are called goslings. What are we? _____

10. I am the top of a mountain. What am I? _____

Long **e** digraphs: Writing words with **ea** or **ee**

Name _____

ea ee

Read each sentence and the word choices.
Choose the word that best completes
each sentence.
Write the word on the line.

1. Brush your _~~teeth~~_____ every day.	**peel** **teeth**
2. A _____ trickled down Clara's cheek.	**heal** **tear**
3. The _____ blue sky had no clouds.	**clear** **beam**
4. I had a _____ about my friend.	**dream** **speak**
5. Please _____ the potatoes.	**feel** **peel**
6. We had _____ stew for dinner.	**leaf** **beef**
7. Chika helped _____ the garden.	**weed** **need**
8. The old door opened with a _____.	**seek** **creak**
9. Riding bikes up the _____ hill was hard.	**deep** **steep**
10. Many kinds of fish live in the _____.	**sea** **see**

Long e digraphs: Completing sentences with **ea** or **ee** words

Name _____

A Key to Long e

In most words, the letter pairs **ie** and **ey** stand for the long **e** sound.

ch<u>ie</u>f   k<u>ey</u>

Read each clue.
Write the best answer or answers using words from the box.

1. Three words that name animals   _____

_____

_____

2. Another word for **leader**   _____

3. A small object that opens a lock   _____

4. An open grassy space   _____

5. Your sister's daughter   _____

6. Someone who steals   _____

7. A part of something   _____

8. Coins or dollars   _____

Word Box				
key	money	collie	monkey	piece
field	chief	niece	thief	donkey

Long e digraphs: Choosing words with **ie** or **ey**

Name _____

Do You See
ie or ey?

Look at each picture.
Choose the word that names the picture.
Write the word on the line.

1. key	**2.**	**3.**
4.	**5.**	**6.**
7.	**8.**	**9.**

Word Box

monkey	key	donkey	money	piece
honey	shield	field	chief	

Long e digraphs: Writing words with ie or ey

Basic Phonics Skills, Level D • EMC 3321 • ©2004 by Evan-Moor Corp.

Name _____

Read each sentence.
Choose the word that best completes each sentence.
Write the word on the line.

1. I put the last _____ of the puzzle in place.

2. Angie found the _____ to the treasure chest.

3. I saw five horses running in the _____.

4. Our dog Trixie is a beautiful _____.

5. Judy took her _____ skating on Saturday.

6. Maya rode a _____ at the petting zoo.

7. I _____ it is very important to be kind.

8. The smoke rose from the _____.

9. How much _____ is in your savings account?

Word Box

money	piece	key	field	chimney
collie	niece	believe	donkey	

Long e digraphs: Completing sentences with ie or ey words

Name _____

I Can Write Sentences

Look at each picture.
Write a sentence about the picture
using the pair of long **e** words.

1.	thief piece
	_____
	_____
2.	weasel donkey
	_____
	_____
3.	seal beep
	_____
	_____
4.	bee honey
	_____
	_____
5.	chimney monkey
	_____
	_____

Long e digraphs: Writing sentences with ea, ee, ie, or ey words

Basic Phonics Skills, Level D • EMC 3321 • ©2004 by Evan-Moor Corp.

Name _____

Do You See Long e Words?

Find each word from the word box
and circle it in the word search.

```
H A N D K E R C H I E F R X
O J I R Z L B O D X L E A P
N C R E A K G O R H E A M D
E Q E A C O M K C B F S P W
Y F K M B Y S I T E E T H E
A S I M O N K E Y L J J H A
T M R I Q R G K T I F Q Y S
L E A V E S N G E E S E P E
Z A S L D H S R V V G H A L
T L T N P I V E M E A T K M
E V E X B E O E W Z U L J W
N W E V D L C N Y A F B X O
U S P E E D M C G W E A V E
```

Word Box

ea		ee	ie	ey
leap	weave	green	believe	honey
leaves	creak	speed	cookie	monkey
meal	dream	steep	shield	
meat	feast	teeth	handkerchief	
weasel		geese		

Review: Long e digraphs

Name _____

A Neat Sheet

Write the word for each picture.
Be aware! Each word will have a long **e** digraph: **ee**, **ea**, **ie**, or **ey**.
Can you spell them correctly?

1.  key _____	2.  _____	3.  _____
4.  _____	5. 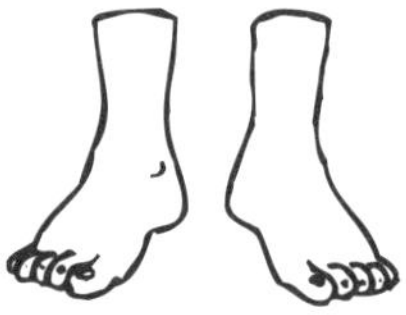 _____	6.  _____
7.  _____	8. 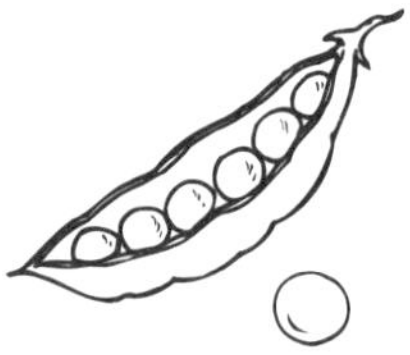 _____	9.  _____
10. 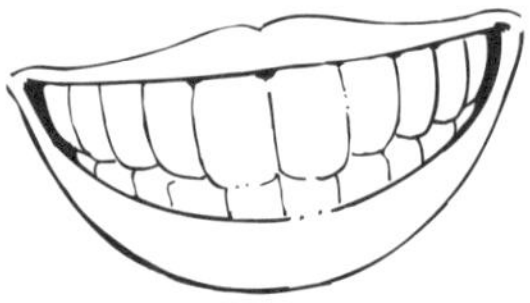 _____	11. 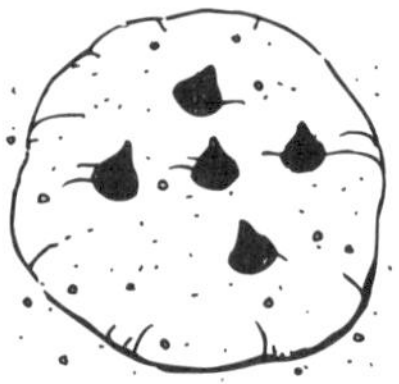 _____	12.  _____

Review: Long e digraphs

Digraphs
Vowel Digraphs

Basic Phonics Skills, Level D • EMC 3321 • ©2004 by Evan-Moor Corp.

Name _____

Bye-Bye!

In some words, the letter pairs **ie**, **uy**, and **ye** stand for the long **i** sound.

p**ie**   b**uy**   b**ye**

Look at each picture.
Circle the word that names each picture.

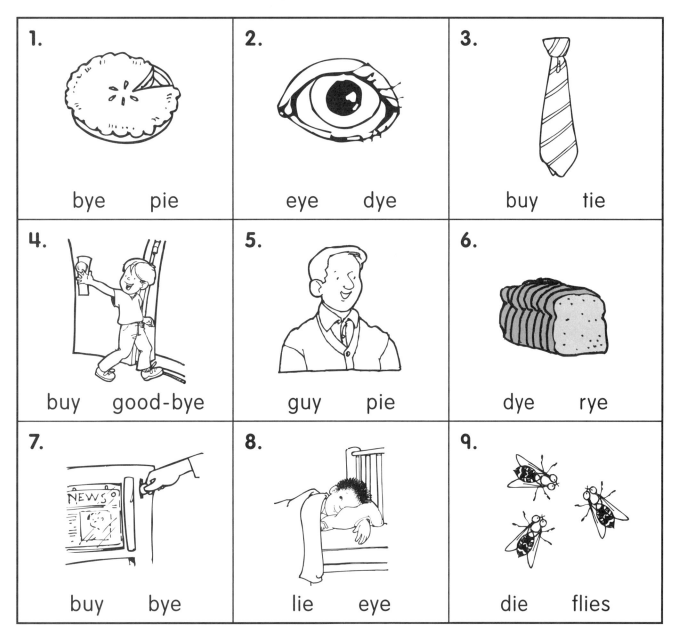

1.
bye   pie

2.
eye   dye

3.
buy   tie

4.
buy   good-bye

5.
guy   pie

6.
dye   rye

7.
buy   bye

8.
lie   eye

9.
die   flies

Long i digraphs: Choosing words with ie, uy, or ye

Name _____

The Guy with a Tie

1. Write the digraph **ie** on the lines to complete each word.

d___ ___   t___ ___

p___ ___   fr___ ___d

l___ ___

2. Write the digraph **uy** on the lines to complete each word.

g___ ___   b___ ___

3. Write the digraph **ye** on the lines to complete each word.

r___ ___   d___ ___   good-b___ ___

4. Write the word that means a kind of pastry.   _____

5. Write the word that means a male person.   _____

6. Write the word that means farewell.   _____

7. Write the word that means a kind of grain.   _____

8. Write the word that means to make a purchase.   _____

Long **i** digraphs: Writing words with **ie**, **uy**, or **ye**

Basic Phonics Skills, Level D • EMC 3321 • ©2004 by Evan-Moor Corp.

Name _____

Missing Words

Choose the word that best completes each sentence.
Write the word on the line.

1. We only need one _____ to play this game.	**die** **buy**
2. Some dirt blew into Helen's _____.	**eyes** **flies**
3. Would you like a slice of apple _____?	**rye** **pie**
4. May _____ her dress blue.	**dyed** **fried**
5. That _____ is a good skier.	**tie** **guy**
6. Please tell your dog to _____ down.	**eye** **lie**
7. This bakery makes dark _____ bread.	**rye** **guy**
8. I am saving my money to _____ a bike.	**buy** **lye**
9. Anita learned to _____ her shoes.	**pie** **tie**
10. We waved _____ as our friends drove away.	**good-bye** **lie**

Long **i** digraphs: Completing sentences with **ie, uy,** or **ye** words

Name _____

Use both of the words together in one sentence.

1.	eye	cried
2.	guy	spies
3.	tried	tie
4.	good-bye	buy
5.	flies	pie

Long i digraphs: Writing sentences with ie, uy, or ye words

Basic Phonics Skills, Level D • EMC 3321 • ©2004 by Evan-Moor Corp.

Name _____

Guy Wants a Pie

Help Guy find the way to the bakery.
Draw a line to follow the path of long **i** words.
You may move up, down, left, or right, but <u>not</u> diagonally.

start

buy	eye	cried	ridge	trick	spin
tin	big	lye	guy	tried	rye
dip	field	bridge	bring	lit	fried
trip	gift	sing	tie	dye	flies
shin	twist	wish	die	pit	will
cliff	zipper	hill	lie	pie	**FINISH**

Review: Long **i** digraphs

©2004 by Evan-Moor Corp. • Basic Phonics Skills, Level D • EMC 3321

Name _____

Long o Digraphs

In some words, the letter pairs **oa**, **oe**, and **ow** stand for the long **o** sound.

bo**at**   **h**oe   **r**ow

Circle the word that names each picture.

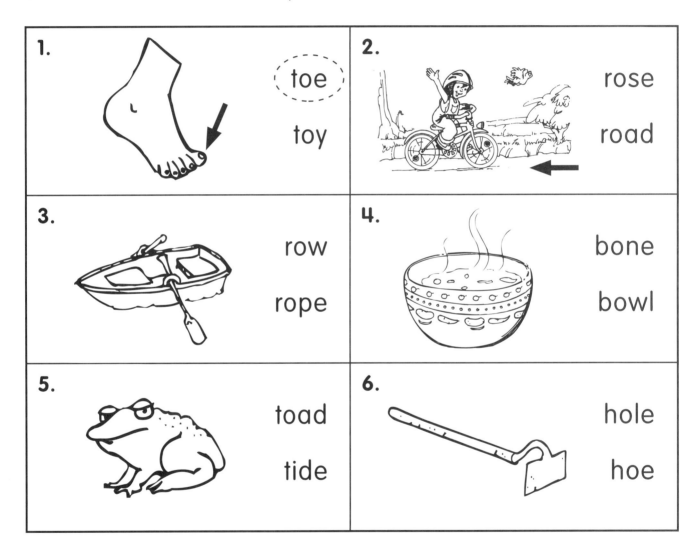

1. toe
   toy

2. rose
   road

3. row
   rope

4. bone
   bowl

5. toad
   tide

6. hole
   hoe

Write the words to complete the sentence.

The bumpy _____ hopped into the _____ boat.

Long **o** digraphs: Choosing words with **oa**, **oe**, or **ow**

Basic Phonics Skills, Level D • EMC 3321 • ©2004 by Evan-Moor Corp.

Name _____

Row by Row

Solve the puzzle using **oa**, **oe**, or **ow** words.

Across
1. to cook in an oven
3. a heavy jacket
4. another word for **sadness**
5. a breakfast grain
7. to plant seeds
8. to place in water for a while
10. the edge of land and water

Down
1. to use an oar
2. five on each foot
3. large black birds
6. heated bread
9. a garden tool
11. flakes in winter

Word Box

coat	woe	toes	snow	soak
crows	hoe	oats	row	
roast	sow	coast	toast	

Long **o** digraphs: Writing words with **oa**, **oe**, or **ow**

Name _____

Show What You Know

Choose the word that best completes each sentence.
Write the word on the line.

1. Mari said, "Please open the _____."

2. A big bowl of hot _____ makes a good breakfast.

3. Therese stubbed her big _____.

4. Ben enjoyed watching the garden plants _____.

5. "The wind is really starting to _____," said Clare.

6. Beth used a red _____ to tie her doll's hair back.

7. Be sure to take a bar of _____ into the shower.

8. We should have turned left at that other _____.

Word Box

toe	grow	bow	oatmeal
blow	window	road	soap

Long **o** digraphs: Completing sentences with **oa**, **oe**, or **ow** words

Name _____

Use both words together in one sentence.

1.		coach	know
		_____	
		_____	
2.		goal	Joan
		_____	
		_____	
3.		moan	groan
		_____	
		_____	
4.		boast	goat
		_____	
		_____	
5.		foe	Joe
		_____	
		_____	

Long o digraphs: Writing sentences with **oa**, **oe**, or **ow** words

Name _____

oa oe ow words

Read each set of words.
One word in each set has a long **o** digraph.
Circle that word.

1. cow
mow
how

2. roast
rod
frost

3. clown
brown
grown

4. growl
brow
blow

5. boat
box
book

6. block
bowl
now

7. soup
soap
soon

8. hook
hoe
honk

9. do
door
doe

Review: Long o digraphs

Name _____

Find the Words Below

Read each sentence.
Underline the **oa**, **oe**, and **ow** long **o** words.
Circle the letters in each word that spell that long **o**.

1. If you play in the <u>snow</u>, please put on your heavy coat.

2. Robert has grown taller than Joe.

3. How tight are your toes in these shoes?

4. Angelica had to mow the lawn before the rain soaked it.

5. After his third bowl of chili, Coach Smith ate some toast.

6. Aimee's dad called for a tow truck on Mulberry Road.

7. The library will loan you a book for two weeks.

8. We made a loaf of bread from wheat we had grown.

9. Joan groaned when she missed the goal.

10. The doe knows when the hunter is near.

Review: Long o digraphs

Name _____

Some New Clues

In some words, the letter pairs **ue**, **ew**, and **eau** stand for the long **u** sound.

bl<u>ue</u>　　**st<u>ew</u>**　　**b<u>eau</u>ty**

Read each clue in the left column.
Find the word in the right column that goes with each clue.
Write the letter for the word on the line.

_d_ **1.** a thick soup

____ **2.** a color

____ **3.** lovely or pretty

____ **4.** to hold together

____ **5.** a precious gem

____ **6.** people as a team

____ **7.** something published
every day

____ **8.** not many

____ **9.** morning moisture

____ **10.** already had information
about something

a. newspaper

b. jewel

c. glue

d. stew

e. knew

f. crew

g. blue

h. beautiful

i. few

j. dew

Long u digraphs: Choosing words with ue, ew, or eau

Basic Phonics Skills, Level D • EMC 3321 • ©2004 by Evan-Moor Corp.

Name _____

A New Crossword

Read each clue.
Write the words to complete the puzzle.

Across

2. a group of people working together
4. to fight with swords
6. bracelets and necklaces
7. what you find in a newspaper
9. not false
10. not many

Down

1. good looks
3. what teeth do to your food
5. the color of the sky on a clear day
8. meat and vegetables cooked together

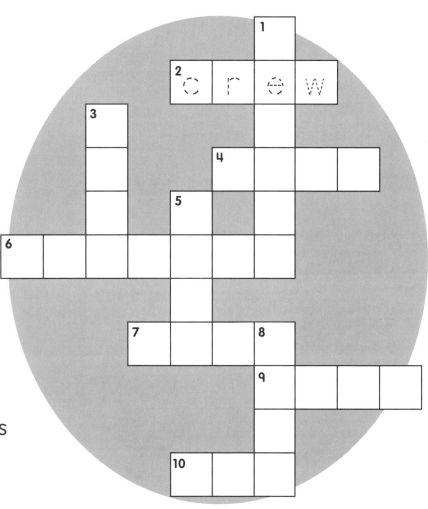

Word Box

beauty	chew	duel	jewelry	stew
blue	crew	few	news	true

Long **u** digraphs: Choosing words with **ue**, **ew**, or **eau**

Name _____

A Few for You

Choose the word that best completes
each sentence.
Write the word on the line.

1. My mother likes to read the morning _____.

2. The famous detective is always looking for _____.

3. My library book is _____ by two days.

4. We need construction paper, _____, and scissors.

5. When Katie released the bird, it _____ away.

6. I _____ I should have studied harder.

7. The outfielder _____ the ball right over his head.

8. Keith _____ the most beautiful pictures of cats.

Word Box

newspaper	drew	threw	clues
knew	flew	glue	overdue

Long u digraphs: Completing sentences with **ue**, **ew**, or **eau** words

Name _____

News for Gwen

Use complete sentences to finish this story.
Use at least 5 of the words from the word box.

In a far-off time, in a far-off land, there lived a lovely young girl named Gwen. Although she was poor, Gwen was very happy. One day, her best friend ran into the cottage. "Gwen!" she exclaimed. "You'll never believe the...

_____

_____

_____

_____

_____

_____

_____

Word Box

news	knew	threw	true
jewelry	drew	blue	untrue
dew	flew	glue	beautiful

Long **u** digraphs: Writing sentences with **ue, ew,** or **eau** words

Build Words

Combine letters from the box with **ue** and **ew**
to make words.

| b | c | d | f | n | bl | cl | gr | gl | tr | thr | scr |

ue	ew

Review: Long **u** digraphs

Basic Phonics Skills, Level D • EMC 3321 • ©2004 by Evan-Moor Corp.

Name _____

Head's Up

The digraph **ea** sometimes stands for the short **e** sound, as in **head**.

Fill in the missing vowels.
Match each picture to its word.

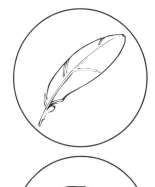

h____ ____d

f____ ____ther

br____ ____d

spr____ ____d

thr____ ____d

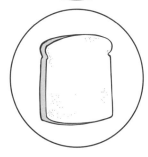

Write the missing words on the lines.

1. Put this _____ in your _____band.

2. _____ the jam on the _____.

3. Use a needle and _____ to fix the rip.

Short vowel digraphs: Choosing words with **ea** /ĕ/

Name _____

New Words Ahead!

ea ui ou
words

Choose the word that best completes
each sentence.
Write the word on the line.

1. My pet _____ is bigger than a hamster.

2. Sara's aunt made a new _____ for her bed.

3. Tricia used a needle and _____ to do her
mending.

4. The sports car zoomed _____ of us.

5. André wants wheat _____ for his sandwich.

6. David's _____ is going to live with his family
for the summer.

7. The meat is so _____ that I can't chew it.

8. Trey wanted a _____ coat for his birthday.

9. Don't _____ the hot stove!

Word Box				
ahead	bread	leather	quilt	tough
touch	thread	guinea pig	cousin	

Short vowel digraphs: Completing sentences with ea /ĕ/, ui /ĭ/, or ou /ŭ/ words

Name _____

Read the words in each box.
Circle the word that has a short vowel sound.

1.
bead
(head)
flea

2.
touch
toast
you

3.
blue
suit
built

4.
quilt
flute
clue

5.
feather
seat
peas

6.
each
ready
reader

7.
rule
roast
rough

8.
treat
thread
tea

9.
count
coat
cue

Review: Short vowel digraphs

Name _____

Healthy, Wealthy, and Wise

ea ui ou words

Write the words to complete the puzzle.

Across

1. the opposite of **city**
3. to construct
4. did a crime
6. plenty
8. rain, snow, wind, temperature
10. used to make a sandwich
12. a stringed instrument
13. to feel with your fingers or hand

Down

1. your aunt's son or daughter
2. the opposite of **old**
5. animal skin used to make shoes
7. on top of your neck
9. not smooth
11. hard to chew

Word Box

touch	build	bread	leather	head
weather	enough	guilty	young	rough
guitar	country	cousin	tough	

Review: Short vowel digraphs

Basic Phonics Skills, Level D • EMC 3321 • ©2004 by Evan-Moor Corp.

Name _____

It's the Law

Phonics Fact!

The digraphs **au** and **aw** stand for the variant sound /ô/.

h**au**nt   s**aw**

Write the word that names the picture.
Circle the letters that say /ô/.

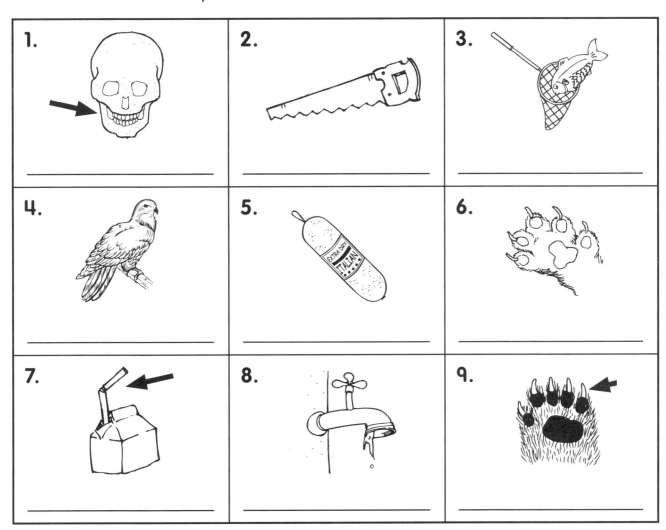

1.

2.

3.

4.

5.

6.

7.

8.

9.

Word Box

straw	claw	jaw	hawk	sausage
paw	saw	caught	faucet	

Variant vowel sound digraphs: Choosing words with **au** or **aw**

Name _____

The Last Straw

Look at each picture.
Write the name of the picture on the line.

1.  _____

2.  _____

3.  _____

4.  _____

5. _____

6.  _____

7.  _____

8.  _____

9. _____

10. _____

Word Box

daughter	saw	crawl	dawn	draw
auto	hawk	straw	claw	paw

Variant vowel sound digraphs: Writing words with au or aw

Basic Phonics Skills, Level D • EMC 3321 • ©2004 by Evan-Moor Corp.

Name _____

Just Learning to Crawl

au aw words

Circle the word that best completes
each sentence.
Write the word on the lines.

1. The baby is learning to _____.	**crawl** **haul**
2. Grandpa drank his lemonade through a _____.	**straw** **draw**
3. That cat's _____ are very sharp!	**pause** **claws**
4. Rover has hurt his _____.	**pause** **paw**
5. Dad's _____ is a dangerous tool.	**scrawl** **saw**
6. I need to _____ some furniture for my mother.	**haul** **raw**
7. I can't believe I _____ that fly ball!	**caught** **taught**
8. Trish says chewing gum makes her _____ hurt.	**paws** **jaws**

Variant vowel sound digraphs: Completing sentences with **au** or **aw** words

Name _____

I Can Write Sentences

Use both words to write a sentence about the picture.

1.		hawk	straw
		_____	
2.		haul	straw
		_____	
3.		fawn	lawn
		_____	
4.		draw	auto
		_____	
5.		crawl	saw
		_____	

Variant vowel sound digraphs: Writing sentences with au or aw words

Basic Phonics Skills, Level D • EMC 3321 • ©2004 by Evan-Moor Corp.

Name _____

Boo!

The vowel digraph **oo** sometimes stands for the sound /$\overline{oo}$/, as in **food**. This is known as the long sound of **oo**.

Look at each picture.
Listen for the vowel sound.
Write the letters **oo** if you hear the /$\overline{oo}$/ sound, as in **food**.

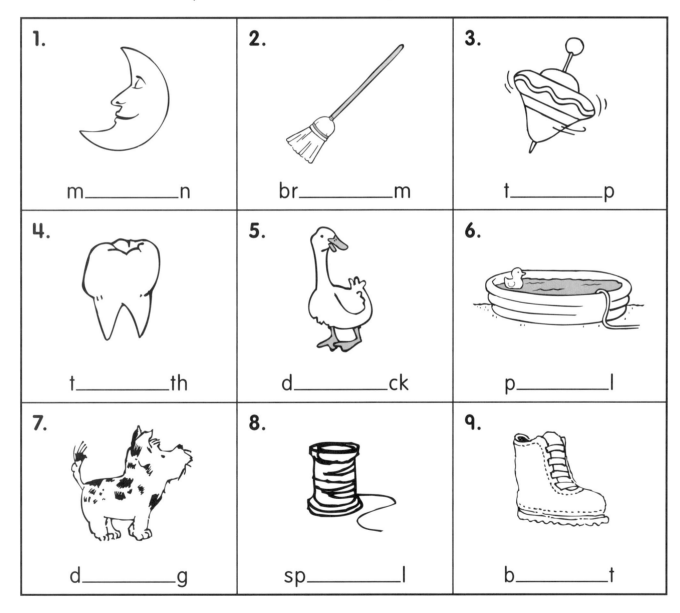

1. m_____n

2. br_____m

3. t_____p

4. t_____th

5. d_____ck

6. p_____l

7. d_____g

8. sp_____l

9. b_____t

Variant vowel sound digraphs: Choosing words with the long sound of oo /$\overline{oo}$/

Name _____

Dinner at the Hood's House

 **Phonics Fact!** The vowel digraph **oo** sometimes stands for the sound /oo/, as in **foot**. This is known as the short sound of **oo**.

Read the story.
Circle each word that has the short sound of **oo**, as in **foot**.
Write each word once on the lines below.

Mr. and Mrs. Hood lived in the woods near a brook. One day, Mrs. Hood said to Mr. Hood, "Please go to the brook and hook some fish for dinner."

Mr. Hood called his dog and they set off for the brook.

Mrs. Hood went to a corner nook to find her cookbook. "I think I'll bake cookies to go with our fish dinner."

She was just taking the cookies out of the oven when she heard, "Woof! Woof!" Next, she heard footsteps on the porch. Mr. Hood was back with two large fish.

That night, the Hoods had a very good dinner.

_____   _____   _____

_____   _____   _____

_____   _____

_____   _____

Variant vowel sound digraphs: Choosing words with the short sound of oo /oo/

Basic Phonics Skills, Level D • EMC 3321 • ©2004 by Evan-Moor Corp.

Name _____

Spoon or Hook?

Read each word.
Listen for the vowel sound of **oo**.
Write each word under either **spoon** or **hook**.

spoon	hook

Word Box

boot	noon	foot	troop
book	tool	brook	cook
zoo	wood	tooth	goose

Variant vowel sound digraphs: Distinguishing between long and short sounds of **oo**

Name _____

Room for Books

Write the word that names each picture.
Underline it if the name has /oo/ as in **hook**.
Circle it if the name has /o͞o/ as in **spoon**.

1. _____

2.  _____

3. _____

4.  _____

5. _____

6. _____

7. _____

8. _____

9. _____

10. _____

11. _____

12. _____

13. _____

14. _____

15. _____

16. _____

Word Box

spoon	foot	book	moon	tooth
cook	wood	moose	hoop	roof
hook	boot	goose	tools	broom

Variant vowel sound digraphs: Writing words with oo

Name _____

Listen for **sh** and **ch**

Write the word that names each picture.
Underline the **ch** or **sh** sound in each word.

1. 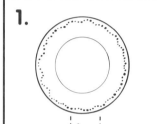 d<u>i</u>sh _____	**2.**  _____	**3.**  _____	**4.**  _____
5.  _____	**6.**  _____	**7.**  _____	**8.**  _____
9.  _____	**10.**  _____	**11.**  _____	**12.** 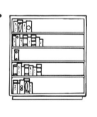 _____

Word Box

shelves	sheep	dish	chair
branch	ship	cheese	shirt
chest	child	chain	shell

Beginning and ending digraphs: **sh, ch**

Name _____

Listen for wh and th

Write the word that names each picture.
Underline the **th** or **wh** sound in each word.

1. thorn	**2.**	**3.**	**4.**
5.	**6.**	**7.**	**8.**
9.	**10.**	**11.** white	**12.**

Word Box

whip	wheel	thumb	thimble
breath	wheat	tooth	whiskers
thorn	north	thirty	white

Beginning and ending digraphs: **th, wh**

Basic Phonics Skills, Level D • EMC 3321 • ©2004 by Evan-Moor Corp.

Name _____

sh, th, ch, wh

Circle the letters that stand for the beginning sound.

1. (sh) th ch wh	2. sh th ch wh	3. sh th ch wh
4. sh th ch wh	5. sh th ch wh	6. sh th ch wh
7. sh th ch wh	8. sh th ch wh	9. sh th ch wh

Circle the word that best completes the sentence.

1. Josh and Cathy went to the _____. **beach** **wish**

2. They took their _____. **rush** **lunch**

3. Each of them had a _____. **wash** **sandwich**

4. They sat on a _____. **bench** **push**

Beginning and ending digraphs: **sh, ch, th, wh**

Name _____

Ming Chin's Shell

Read each pair of sentences.
Choose the word that best completes
each sentence.

1. The fog was _____*thick*_____. Ming Chin heard the _____.	**whistle** **thick**
2. She did not see the _____. She did not know _____ it would come.	**ship** **when**
3. She held a _____ in her hand. It helped to _____ her up.	**cheer** **shell**
4. _____ had a long way to go. The shell was on a gold _____.	**chain** **She**
5. She would _____ it to her new family. She would tell _____ about China.	**them** **show**

Beginning and ending digraphs: **sh, ch, th, wh**

Basic Phonics Skills, Level D • EMC 3321 • ©2004 by Evan-Moor Corp.

Name _____

Listen for f

Sometimes the digraphs **ph** and **gh** stand for the /f/ sound.

rou<u>gh</u>   <u>ph</u>antom

Write the word that names the picture.
Underline **ph** or **gh**. Circle where you hear the sound.

1.  ~~photo~~ _____   (beginning)   middle   end

2. _____   beginning   middle   end

3. _____   beginning   middle   end

4. _____   beginning   middle   end

5. _____   beginning   middle   end

6. _____   beginning   middle   end

7. _____   beginning   middle   end

8. _____   beginning   middle   end

Word Box

phone	laugh	graph	gopher
photo	pheasant	cough	trophy

Writing **/f/** digraphs: **ph, gh**

Some Tough Clues

 **Phonics Fact!** The digraph **ph** stands for the /f/ sound wherever it appears. The digraph **gh** stands for the /f/ sound when it appears at the end of a word.

Circle the word that matches the clue.
Write the word on the line.
Underline **ph** or **gh**.

1. It rings
enough   photo   (phone)   _phone_

2. You look at this
laugh   photo   cough   _____

3. You do this when you have a cold
cough   tough   phase   _____

4. Hard to chew
phone   tough   photo   _____

5. The right amount
enough   phonics   pheasant   _____

6. Not smooth
phantom   rough   enough   _____

7. A wild bird
phone   pheasant   cough   _____

8. Not real
phony   photo   rough   _____

Writing **/f/** digraphs: **ph, gh**

Name _____

Did Phil Phone Home?

The digraph **ph** stands for the /f/ sound wherever it appears. The digraph **gh** stands for the /f/ sound when it appears at the end of a word.

Underline the sentence that fits the picture.
Write the **ph** or **gh** word or words in that sentence on the lines.

1.

   The road is rough.   rough _____

   The road makes him cough.   _____

2.

   That phone is funny.   _____

   That joke made Phil laugh.   _____

                                 _____

3.

   The phone call made her laugh. _____

   She likes photos.   _____

                                 _____

4.

   Phyllis has a bad phone.   _____

   She has a bad cough.   _____

                                 _____

Review: The /f/ digraphs ph and gh

Diphthongs

Name _____

oi or oy?

A **diphthong** is a vowel pair in which two sounds slide together. The vowel pairs **oi** and **oy** stand for the /oi/ sound.

soil   use **oi** in the middle of the word
toy   use **oy** at the end of the word

Say the name of each picture.
Write the letters **oi** or **oy** on the lines.
Fill in the circle that shows where you hear the sound.

1.	● beginning ○ middle ○ end ____ ____ l	**2.**	○ beginning ○ middle ○ end b____ ____
3.	○ beginning ○ middle ○ end s____ ____ l	**4.**	○ beginning ○ middle ○ end c____ ____ l
5.	○ beginning ○ middle ○ end t____ ____	**6.**	○ beginning ○ middle ○ end c____ ____ns
7.	○ beginning ○ middle ○ end b____ ____ l	**8.**	○ beginning ○ middle ○ end p____ ____nt

Diphthongs: Choosing words with the /oi/ sound spelled oi or oy

Name _____

The Joy of Toys

Read each riddle.
Choose the best answer.
Write the word on the line.

1. I am dangerous to eat or drink.   _poison_

2. You'll find these in a change purse.   _____

3. I am another word for **happy**.   _____

4. I am a shellfish.   _____

5. I am fun to play with.   _____

6. I am the sharp end of a pencil.   _____

7. I am a trip over the water.   _____

8. I am more than one option.   _____

9. I am another word for **ruin**.   _____

10. I am a male child.   _____

11. I am another word for **dirt**.   _____

12. I am what happens when you heat liquid. _____

Word Box

oyster	toys	point	choice
joyful	boil	boy	voyage
coins	poison	destroy	soil

Diphthongs: Writing words with the /oi/ sound spelled **oi** or **oy**

Name _____

Loyal to Royalty

Read each sentence.
Choose the word that best completes
each sentence.
Write the word on the line.

1. The princess used the _____
   to make her skin soft.

2. All of the young men wanted to _____
   the king's army.

3. The king _____ to the men he thought
   were brave.

4. He was afraid his kingdom would be _____ by his
   enemies.

5. He promised a gold _____ to any man who protected
   the kingdom.

6. They all raised their _____ to cheer for the good king.

7. The princess had to make a _____ of which man
   to marry.

8. Rob Roy felt _____ when she chose him.

Word Box			
pointed	oil	join	joyful
choice	voices	destroyed	coin

Diphthongs: Completing sentences with **oi** or **oy** words

Name _____

I Can Write Sentences

Use both words in a sentence that tells about the picture.

1.	boy	coins
2.	coiled	soil
3.	toy	noise
4.	oil	joint
5.	joy	point

Diphthongs: Writing sentences with oi or oy words

Basic Phonics Skills, Level D • EMC 3321 • ©2004 by Evan-Moor Corp.

Name _____

A Cow in the House

A **diphthong** is a vowel pair in which two sounds slide together. The vowel pairs **ou** and **ow** stand for the /ou/ sound.

o<u>u</u>t   **c<u>ow</u>**

Look at the picture.
Find the picture name in the list of words.
Write the letter for the word on the line.

____ 1.    **a.** mouth

____ 2.   **b.** couch

____ 3.   **c.** cow

____ 4.   **d.** hour

____ 5.   **e.** brown

____ 6.   **f.** clown

____ 7.   **g.** cloud

____ 8.   **h.** flour

____ 9.   **i.** house

____ 10.   **j.** mouse

Diphthongs: Choosing words with the /ou/ sound spelled ou or ow

Name _____

ou or ow?

Write the missing letters to name each picture.
Change the first letter or letters to form a new word.
Write the new word in the next box.

1.		c __ o __ w	h o w
2.		h_____ _____se	
3.		c_____ _____ch	
4.		m_____ _____th	
5.		g_____ _____n	
6.		s_____ _____r	
7.		cl_____ _____d	
8.		b_____ _____nce	
9.		fl_____ _____r	
10.		sc_____ _____t	

Diphthongs: Writing words with the /ou/ sound spelled ou or ow

Basic Phonics Skills, Level D • EMC 3321 • ©2004 by Evan-Moor Corp.

Name _____

The Circus Came to Town

Use complete sentences to finish this story.
Use at least 7 of the words from the word box.
The story has been started for you.

Anna

Anna enjoyed hanging out with her friends. But that changed the day the circus came to town.

_____

_____

_____

_____

_____

_____

_____

Word Box					
town	mouse	brown	sound	crowd	about
clown	hour	found	frown	out	around

Diphthongs: Writing sentences with **ou** or **ow** words /ou/

Name _____

Read the underlined word in each sentence. Change the beginning letter or letters to make the word that best completes the sentence. Write the new word on the line.

1. The <u>mouse</u> ran into the _____ house _____.

2. Please don't <u>slouch</u> on the _____.

3. It took an <u>hour</u> to sift all the wheat _____.

4. The <u>cow</u> pulled the farmer's old _____.

5. I wore my new <u>gown</u> at the dance in our _____.

6. The cat <u>bounced</u> off the couch and _____ on the mouse.

7. I <u>found</u> a penny on the _____.

8. <u>Now</u> is the time to learn _____ to swim.

9. That loud <u>sound</u> was _____ to upset the neighbors.

10. The sad <u>clown</u> wore a _____ on his face.

Diphthongs: Completing sentences with **ou** or **ow** words /ou/

Name _____

Sound It Out

Remember: A **diphthong** has two vowel sounds that blend together.

s<u>oi</u>l   **t<u>oy</u>**   **<u>ou</u>t**   **c<u>ow</u>**

Read the words in each box.
Listen for the vowel sound in each word.
Circle the word or words that have the diphthong sound /**oi**/ or /**ou**/.

1.	2.	3.
moth (oil) (brown)	boy hope corn	own coil town

4.	5.	6.
follow below mouth	gown point rose	country joy count

7.	8.	9.
mouse most moist	cousin coin core	ground grow growl

Review: Diphthongs oi, oy, ou, ow

Name _____

Review

Each word is missing a vowel pair.
Fill in the blanks with the letters **oi**, **oy**, **ou**, or **ow** to complete each word.

1. m____ ____se	**2.** cl____ ____n	**3.** c____ ____ns
4. g____ ____n	**5.** b____ ____	**6.** tr____ ____t
7. s____ ____l	**8.** cl____ ____d	**9.** c____ ____
10. t____ ____	**11.** h____ ____se	**12.** m____ ____th

Review: Diphthongs oi, oy, ou, ow

R-Controlled Vowels

Name _____

Not So Hard to Do

Read each clue.
Write the correct letter or letters to complete the answer.

h	c	st	sm	l	p	f	h	d	ch

1. A place where crops and animals are raised   __f__arm

2. To cause hurt or damage   ____arm

3. A lucky item   ____ ____arm

4. To begin   ____ ____art

5. A small, sharp object you throw at a target   ____art

6. Intelligent   ____ ____art

7. Some, but not all; a piece   ____art

8. A kind of shortening made from animal fat   ____ard

9. The opposite of **soft**   ____ard

10. You send this to say Happy Birthday   ____ard

Chunking/writing more words in the **ar** family /är/: **-ard, -art, -arm**

Basic Phonics Skills, Level D • EMC 3321 • ©2004 by Evan-Moor Corp.

Name _____

Pick a Card

Read the **ar** words. Read each riddle.
Write the word on the line that answers the riddle.

March

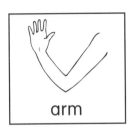
arm

artist

barn

cart

market

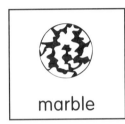
marble

carpet

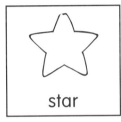
star

bark

1. I am a place where you buy things. _market_

2. I am a person who paints pictures. _____

3. I am a month of the year. _____

4. I am useful to move things. _____

5. I am a floor covering. _____

6. I am a sound dogs make. _____

7. I am a part of the body. _____

8. I am a building where farm animals live. _____

9. I am a twinkling object. _____

10. I am a small ball made of glass. _____

Writing **ar** words to complete sentences

Name _____

Chart Each Part

Read each sentence.
Fill in the puzzle with the **ar** word that completes the sentence.

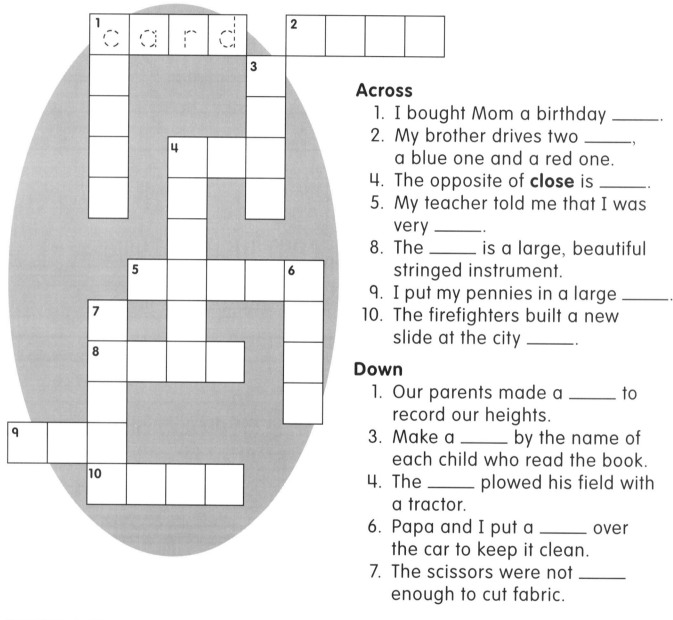

Across

1. I bought Mom a birthday _____.
2. My brother drives two _____, a blue one and a red one.
4. The opposite of **close** is _____.
5. My teacher told me that I was very _____.
8. The _____ is a large, beautiful stringed instrument.
9. I put my pennies in a large _____.
10. The firefighters built a new slide at the city _____.

Down

1. Our parents made a _____ to record our heights.
3. Make a _____ by the name of each child who read the book.
4. The _____ plowed his field with a tractor.
6. Papa and I put a _____ over the car to keep it clean.
7. The scissors were not _____ enough to cut fabric.

Word Box

park	tarp	card	sharp	farmer	mark
harp	jar	chart	smart	far	cars

Writing **ar** words to complete sentences

Basic Phonics Skills, Level D • EMC 3321 • ©2004 by Evan-Moor Corp.

Name _____

I Can Write Sentences

Read each pair of **ar** words.
Write a sentence using both words.

1.	shark	guitar
	_____	
	_____	
2.	park	cart
	_____	
	_____	
3.	farmer	garden
	_____	
	_____	
4. PLEASE COME	card	party
	_____	
	_____	
5.	star	charm
	_____	
	_____	

Writing sentences with ar words

Name _____

3 Ways to Spell It

Phonics Fact!

The /âr/ sound can be spelled three ways:

ch<u>air</u>   **c<u>are</u>**   **b<u>ear</u>**

Say the name of each picture.
Add the beginning letter or letters to complete the word.

1. ____air

2. ____air

3. ____air

4. ____ ____airs

5. ____are

6. ____ear

7. ____ear

8. ____ ____are

9. ____ ____are

Chunking words with the /âr/ sound: -air, -are, or -ear

Name _____

A Scary Night

Read each sentence.
Fill in the circle by the word that best completes
the sentence.
Write the word on the line.

1. We all came down the _____stairs_____ at 8:00.
  ○ **pair**   ● **stairs**   ○ **share**

2. It is _____ that we are all home
  on a Friday night.
  ○ **rare**   ○ **pear**   ○ **stare**

3. Mom brought a _____ of popcorn bowls.
  ○ **hair**   ○ **flare**   ○ **pair**

4. I knew the monster movie would _____ my sister.
  ○ **care**   ○ **scare**   ○ **share**

5. I had to _____ her to keep her eyes open.
  ○ **square**   ○ **stairs**   ○ **dare**

6. The monster was so big, all I could do was _____ at it.
  ○ **stare**   ○ **fair**   ○ **pear**

7. At the end, the monster went into his dark _____ to hide.
  ○ **dare**   ○ **rare**   ○ **lair**

8. The people made a sign that read "_____ of monster!"
  ○ **Wear**   ○ **Beware**   ○ **Repair**

Choosing **air, are,** or **ear** words to complete sentences /ar/

Name _____

Lucky Charm

Read each sentence.
Choose the correct word ending from the pair provided.
Circle the ending to complete the word.
Write the whole word on the line.

1. Do you have a lucky ch_____?   ___charm___

(-arm)   or   -art

2. The m_____ won the horse race.   _____

-are   or   -ark

3. Our last math test was very h_____.   _____

-ear   or   -ard

4. When does José st_____ his new job?   _____

-art   or   -are

5. Mom said, "Please w_____ your jacket."   _____

-arm   or   -ear

6. This p_____ is sweet and juicy.   _____

-ear   or   -ark

7. Hiro and Manuel sh_____ a room
in the dorm.   _____

-ark   or   -are

8. Selma's d_____ hit the bull's-eye.   _____

-art   or   -are

Review: Words with the /är/ or /âr/ sound

Name _____

Stare at the Stars

Choose the word that best completes each sentence.
Write the word on the line.

1. Mark's dog likes to _____.

   bark   **bear**

2. That movie will _____ my little sister.

   scar   **scare**

3. Dad put the _____ tire on the car.

   spar   **spare**

4. Polluted water can _____ fish.

   harm   **hare**

5. We looked at the _____ through a telescope.

   stars   **stares**

6. The snowshoe _____ turns white in the winter.

   harp   **hare**

7. The lost hikers shot a _____ into the air.

   flare   **far**

8. Mato takes very good _____ of his new puppy.

   car   **care**

9. Our family likes to play _____ on Saturday night.

   cards   **cares**

10. Meg needs a _____ of skates that fit her.

    part   **pair**

Review: Words with the /är/ or /âr/ sound

Name _____

The Power of r

When the vowel **e** is followed by the letter **r**, the **r** changes the sound of the vowel.

h<u>er</u>

Read each clue.
Choose the correct beginning letter or letters and write them on the lines.

h	f	g	h	j	t	v	cl	st	h

1. A plant used to flavor food   h ___erb

2. An action word   ____erb

3. A length of time   ____erm

4. It can cause disease   ____erm

5. A sudden movement   ____erk

6. A salesperson in a store   ____ ____erk

7. A frilly green plant   ____ern

8. A group of horses or cows   ____erd

9. A pronoun for a girl or woman   ____er

10. Harsh or firm   ____ ____ern

Chunking words with the /ûr/ sound: - er, - erb, - erd, - erk, - erm, - ern

Name _____

No One Is Perfect

Read each phrase.
Choose the word that best completes each phrase.
Circle the letters **er** in the word.

perfect

1. A _____ score

_____

2. Orange or lime _____

_____

3. A _____ in a cage

_____

4. The little _____ in the sea

_____

5. _____ not to forget

_____

6. A game of _____

_____

7. _____ about giving a speech

_____

8. The king's personal _____

_____

9. A _____ in the courtroom

_____

10. A _____ of cattle

_____

Word Box

checkers	perfect	sherbet	mermaid	gerbil
lawyer	nervous	herd	remember	servant

Writing words with the /ûr/ sound: - er, - erb, - erd, - erm

Name _____

The Third Bird

Read each clue.
Write in the missing letter or letters to complete the word.

b	f	g	s	st	th	tw	f

1. A feathered animal   __b__ird

2. After second   _____ _____ird

3. A kind of evergreen tree   _____ir

4. You do this with a spoon   _____ _____ir

5. A title of respect for a man   _____ir

6. A young female person   _____irl

7. To spin around   _____ _____irl

8. Quite hard   _____irm

Chunking words with the /ûr/ sound: -ir, -ird, -irl, -irm

Name _____

Make New Words

Write word chunks on each line to create new words.

-irt	-irst
d_dirt_____	f_____
sh_____	th_____
sk_____	
squ_____	

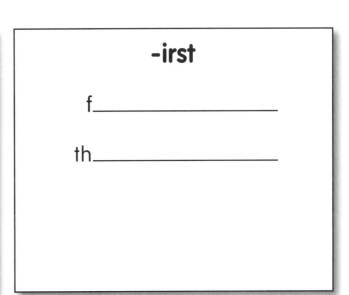

Choose a word from above that best answers each clue.

1. A feeling of needing something to drink   _____

2. Another name for **soil**   _____

3. Clothing with sleeves   _____

4. Before second   _____

5. Clothing a girl wears   _____

6. What you do with a water gun   _____

Name _____

Does a Turtle Hurry?

Phonics Fact!

When the vowel **u** is followed by the letter **r**, the **r** changes the sound of the vowel.

f**ur**   b**ur**n   c**ur**b

Fill in the missing letter to complete the answer to each clue.

f   t   h   f   b   p   n   t

1. An animal's hair   f___ur

2. The sound made by a happy cat   ___urr

3. What fire does   ___urn

4. To be in a rush   ___urry

5. Works at a hospital   ___urse

6. A root vegetable   ___urnip

7. Table and chair   ___urniture

8. A reptile with a hard shell   ___urtle

Chunking/writing words with the /ûr/ sound: -ur, -urb, -urn

Name _____

The Curse of the Nurse's Purse

Read the story.
Underline each word that has the letters **ur**.
Then use those words to solve the clues below.

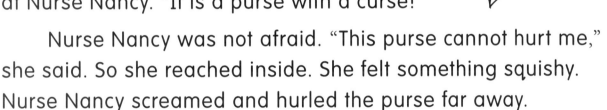

    <u>Nurse</u> Nancy needed a new purse. She went to the store. "It won't hurt to look here," she thought. So she combed her curls and walked in.

    "What do you want?" asked a clerk.

    "I want a new purse," said the nurse.

    "Well, I have just the purse for you," the clerk blurted out. And she threw an old purse at Nurse Nancy. "It is a purse with a curse!"

    Nurse Nancy was not afraid. "This purse cannot hurt me," she said. So she reached inside. She felt something squishy. Nurse Nancy screamed and hurled the purse far away.

    What was in the purse, you ask?

    It was just yogurt!

1. Someone who takes care of the sick   _____

2. A dairy product   _____

3. It holds a woman's personal items   _____

4. An evil spell   _____

5. To cause pain   _____

6. To say suddenly   _____

Chunking/writing words with the /ûr/ sound: **-url, -urse, -urt**

Name _____

No Turnips for Her

er ir ur words

Read each sentence.
Fill in the circle by the word that best
completes the sentence.
Write the word on the line.

1. Janice had ten candles on her ___birthday___ cake.
   ○ **thirsty**   ● **birthday**

2. The weather man predicts snow _____
   for tonight.
                ○ **flurries**   ○ **blur**

3. The dancers _____ across the floor.
                ○ **twirled**   ○ **third**

4. Omar got a _____ score on his spelling test.
                ○ **termite**   ○ **perfect**

5. A _____ is a fairy-tale creature.
                ○ **turnip**   ○ **mermaid**

6. We bought new _____ for the living room.
                ○ **purse**   ○ **furniture**

7. Nancy had to _____ to avoid hitting the deer.
                ○ **swerve**   ○ **burp**

8. A powerful _____ swept across Florida.
                ○ **hurricane**   ○ **churn**

9. The girl eats _____ for breakfast.
                ○ **yogurt**   ○ **dirt**

Writing words with the /ûr/ sound to complete sentences

Basic Phonics Skills, Level D • EMC 3321 • ©2004 by Evan-Moor Corp.

Name _____

I Can Write Sentences

Look at each picture.
Read the pair of words.
Use both words to write a sentence about the picture.

1. 	turn	curve
2. 	squirt	shirt
3. 	thirsty	person
4. 	clerk	purse
5. 	third	skirt

Writing sentences using words with the /ûr/ sound

R-Controlled Vowels 161

Name _____

Riddle Fun
or words

Read each clue.
Use the letter tiles to fill in the missing letters.

b   c   f   p   t   sc   st   c

1. Covered area on a house

p	o	r	c	h

2. Used with a spoon

	o	r	k

3. Meat from a pig

	o	r	k

4. Used to close a bottle

	o	r	k

5. A rope or twine

	o	r	d

6. The edge or boundary

	o	r	d	e	r

7. A fire light carried by hand

	o	r	c	h

8. A large bird with long legs

		o	r	k

9. To burn a little

		o	r	c	h

Chunking/writing words with the /ôr/ sound: -orch, -ord, -ork

Basic Phonics Skills, Level D • EMC 3321 • ©2004 by Evan-Moor Corp.

Name _____

Form Words

1. Write the chunk **-orm** on each line to make a word.

d<u>orm</u>_____   st_____

f_____   n_____al

2. Write the chunk **-orn** on each line to make a word.

b_____   c_____

t_____   w_____

3. Write the chunk **-ort** on each line to make a word.

f_____   sh_____

sp_____   s_____

4. Use the words above to solve each clue.

A kind of grain   _____

A game or contest   _____

The opposite of **tall**   _____

Ripped   _____

Wind and rain   _____

Chunking/writing words with the /ôr/ sound: -orm, -orn, -ort

Name _____

Make New Words

When the vowel **o** or vowel pairs with **o** are followed by the letter **r**, the **r** usually changes the vowel sound.

f<u>or</u>   **s<u>oar</u>**

1. Write the chunk **-or** on the line to complete each word.

f <u>or</u>_____   n_____

2. Write the chunk **-oar** on the line to complete each word.

b_____   s_____   r_____

3. Write the chunk **-oor** on the line to complete each word.

d_____   fl_____

4. Write the chunk **-our** on the line to complete each word.

f_____   p_____

Write the word from above that names each picture.

 1. _____   4. _____

2. _____   5. _____

 3. _____    6. _____

Chunking/writing words with the /ôr/ sound: **-or, -oar, -oor, -ore, -our**

Name _____

Score Four More!

Write the chunk **-ore** on the line to complete each word.

1. b ̅o̅r̅e̅ _____

2. c _____

3. sh _____

4. m _____

5. t _____

6. st _____

7. sc _____

8. sn _____

9. w _____

10. ch _____

Write the word from above that names each picture.

1.  _____	**2.**  _____	**3.**  _____
4.  _____	**5.**  _____	**6.** 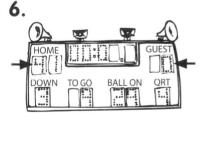 _____

Chunking/writing words with the /ôr/ sound

Name _____

Where Does It Go?

Read each word in the word box.
Listen for the vowel sound.
Write the word under the heading where it belongs.

/är/ as in **car**	/âr/ as in **chair**
star	
/ûr/ as in girl	**/ôr/ as in corn**

Word Box

cord	curl	fur	worn	farm
turtle	star	pair	hair	pour
yard	storm	germ	door	scare
pear	bear	square	smart	large
store	dirt	dark	shirt	

Review: R-controlled vowel sounds

Name _____

Word Search

ar, er, ir, or, ur

There are 20 words in this grid that contain an **r**-controlled vowel. Find each word and circle it.

```
S  Q  U  I  R  T  C  F  S
O  A  G  S  H  A  R  P  H
R  C  A  R  T  R  B  U  O
E  L  K  P  V  P  A  R  R
G  E  R  M  E  H  R  P  T
I  R  M  D  R  O  K  L  H
R  K  H  I  B  R  L  E  S
L  D  A  R  K  N  B  O  P
E  Q  R  T  O  R  N  D  O
J  S  P  O  R  C  H  I  R
S  T  O  R  K  N  T  R  T
```

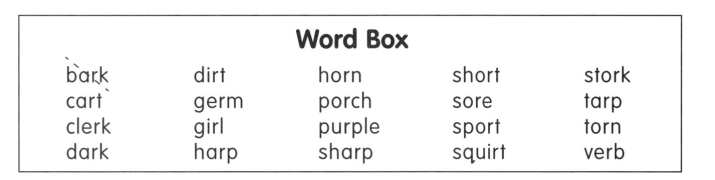

Word Box

bark	dirt	horn	short	stork
cart	germ	porch	sore	tarp
clerk	girl	purple	sport	torn
dark	harp	sharp	squirt	verb

Review: R-controlled vowel sounds

Name _____

Name the 20 objects below.
Write the name of each object on the line.

1.  _____

2. _____

3. _____

4.  _____

5. _____

6.  _____

7. _____

8.  _____

9. _____

10.  _____

11. _____

12. _____

13. _____

14. _____

15.  _____

16. _____

17.  _____

18. _____

19. _____

20. _____

Review: R-controlled vowel sounds

Syllables and Schwa

BASIC Phonics Skills

Name _____

Is It a Syllable?

Phonics Fact!

A **syllable** is a word part that contains one vowel sound. The number of vowel sounds in a word equal the number of syllables.

  cat = one vowel sound /ă/ = one syllable
  picnic = two vowel sounds /ĭ/ and /ĭ/ = two syllables

Read each word.
Listen to the underlined portion of the word.
If you hear a vowel sound, it is a syllable.

Is it a syllable?

1.		**ba**by	⬤ yes	◯ no
2.		**tr**ee	◯ yes	◯ no
3.		**cat**	◯ yes	◯ no
4.		wa**gon**	◯ yes	◯ no
5.		**bas**ket	◯ yes	◯ no
6.		clo**wn**	◯ yes	◯ no
7.		pu**pp**y	◯ yes	◯ no
8.		**can**dle	◯ yes	◯ no
9.		**cup**	◯ yes	◯ no
10.		**pen**cil	◯ yes	◯ no

Distinguishing a syllable from a nonsyllable

Basic Phonics Skills, Level D • EMC 3321 • ©2004 by Evan-Moor Corp.

Name _____

How Many Sounds?

The number of vowel <u>letters</u> and the number of vowel <u>sounds</u> in a word may not be the same.

tree = <u>2</u> vowel letters (**e** and **e**) but only <u>1</u> vowel sound

Circle the vowel letters in each word.
Read each word and count the vowel sounds you hear.
Write the number of syllables in the box.

Syllables

1. phone [ ]

2. flowers [ ]

3. calendar [ ]

4. alligator [ ]

5. kitten [ ]

6. watch [ ]

7. computer [ ]

Syllables

8. dinosaur [ ]

9. book [ ]

10. radio [ ]

11. finger [ ]

12. feather [ ]

13. football [ ]

14. throne [ ]

Counting the number of vowel sounds in a word

Name _____

Vowel Sounds and Syllables

 **Phonics Fact!** Remember: A **syllable** is a word part that contains one vowel sound. The number of vowel <u>sounds</u> in a word = the number of syllables.

Listen for the vowel sounds.
Count the syllables in each word.
Write the words in the correct box.

1 syllable	2 syllables
rose	
3 syllables	**4 syllables**

Word Box

rose	fifteen	telephone
castle	California	swing
ladder	supermarket	doughnut

Counting syllables in a word (1, 2, 3, 4 syllables)

Basic Phonics Skills, Level D • EMC 3321 • ©2004 by Evan-Moor Corp.

Name _____

Divide Them Up

Phonics Fact!

Words can be divided into parts by syllable. When two or more consonants appear in the middle of a word, the word is usually divided between them.

pic•nic   **din•ner**

Divide each word into syllables.
The first two have been done for you.

1. captain ___cap•tain___

2. coffee ___cof•fee___

3. sister _____

4. shepherd _____

5. fountain _____

6. penny _____

7. party _____

8. runner _____

9. silly _____

10. basket _____

11. plastic _____

12. swimming _____

13. platter _____

14. silver _____

15. mistake _____

16. angel _____

Dividing VCCV words

Name _____

Long and Short

Divide each word into two syllables.

1. begin

2. table _____

3. music _____

4. radar _____

5. spider _____

6. minus _____

7. robot _____

8. open _____

Divide each word into two syllables.

1. planet

2. comet _____

3. money _____

4. wizard _____

5. cabin _____

6. honey _____

7. jungle _____

8. number _____

Dividing words: VCV words (long and short vowels)

Name _____

A Little Syllable

Phonics Fact!

When a word ends in a consonant plus **-le**, divide the word before the consonant.

ta•ble   **pud•dle**

Read each word.
Divide the word into two syllables.

1. candle _can•dle_

2. cable _____

3. turtle _____

4. thistle _____

5. cradle _____

6. thimble _____

7. people _____

8. marble _____

9. bubble _____

10. puddle _____

11. apple _____

12. needle _____

13. eagle _____

14. rattle _____

15. maple _____

16. handle _____

Dividing words: Words with **-le**

Name _____

Try This!

Underline the **le** in each word.
Then divide each word into syllables.
Do you remember the rule?

1. circle cir•cle _____	**2.** sparkle _____	**3.** simple _____
4. double _____	**5.** tumble _____	**6.** puzzle _____
7. uncle _____	**8.** tremble _____	**9.** gentle _____
10. wiggle _____	**11.** purple _____	**12.** vehicle _____

Dividing words: Words with -le

   Basic Phonics Skills, Level D • EMC 3321 • ©2004 by Evan-Moor Corp.

Name _____

Calling All Pilots!

When a word has more than one syllable, one of the syllables is stressed. That syllable is marked with an accent mark (').

pi'•lot

Divide each word into two syllables.
Mark the stressed syllable with an accent mark (').
Circle the unstressed syllable.

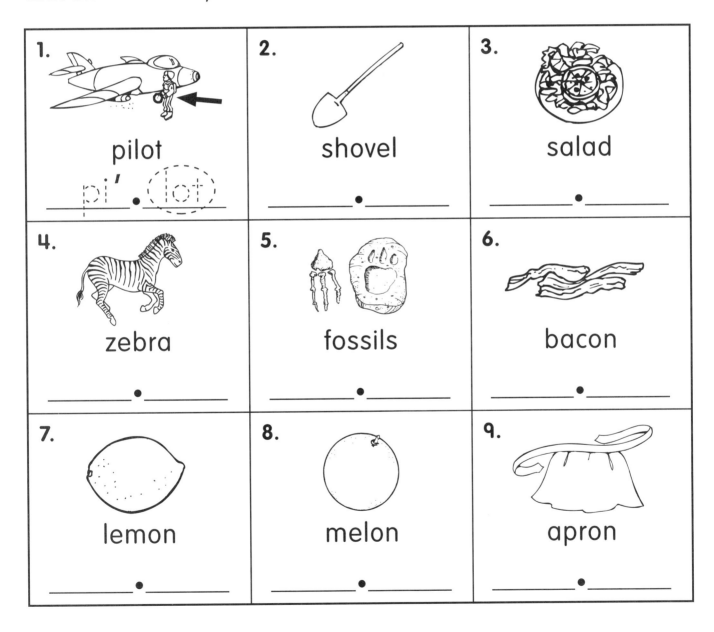

1. pilot
   pi' • lot

2. shovel
   ____ • ____

3. salad
   ____ • ____

4. zebra
   ____ • ____

5. fossils
   ____ • ____

6. bacon
   ____ • ____

7. lemon
   ____ • ____

8. melon
   ____ • ____

9. apron
   ____ • ____

Choosing the unstressed syllable with the schwa sound

Name _____

Use Your Colored Pencils

Phonics Fact! The vowel in an unstressed syllable will usually have the /u/ sound. This is called the **schwa** sound and is marked as ə.

Each word is divided into syllables.
Color the unstressed syllable.
That is the syllable that has the schwa vowel sound.

1. | a | way |

8. | piz | za |

2. | a | bout |

9. | ap | ple |

3. | bal | loon |

10. | met | al |

4. | so | fa |

11. | but | ton |

5. | doz | en |

12. | bub | ble |

6. | per | son |

13. | fi | nal |

7. | pen | cil |

14. | pa | rade |

Choosing the unstressed syllable with the schwa sound

Basic Phonics Skills, Level D • EMC 3321 • ©2004 by Evan-Moor Corp.

Name _____

The Written Word

Look at each picture.
Write the word that names the picture.
Circle the syllable that has the schwa sound.

1. 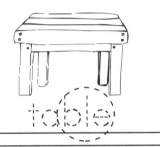  _____	**2.**  _____	**3.**  _____
4.  _____	**5.**  _____	**6.** _____
7.  _____	**8.**  _____	**9.**  _____

Word Box

robin	tàble	barrel
pizza	nickel	pencil
balloon	bacon	wagon

Writing words with the schwa sound

Name _____

Final Answer

Phonics Fact! The vowel in an unstressed syllable will usually have the /u/ sound. This is called the **schwa** sound and is marked as ə.

Choose the word that best completes each sentence.
Write the word on the line.
Circle the schwa sound in each word.

1. Marcus wants to sew a _____ button _____ on his shirt.

2. "Take out a sheet of paper and a _____," the teacher said.

3. Winter is Tommie's favorite _____.

4. The beautiful princess lived in a _____.

5. If you hike in the desert, look for a _____.

6. When Sue broke her arm, we took her to the _____.

7. We need another _____ for the game.

8. Would you please set the _____ for dinner?

9. Someday, Cindy may become a _____ singer.

Word Box

button	famous	pencil
hospital	table	season
person	palace	cactus

Completing sentences with words that have the schwa sound

Name _____

Gerbils on Parade

Anika's gerbils are loose!
Write a story about Anika and her gerbils.
Use at least 6 of the words from the word box.

_____

_____

_____

_____

_____

_____

_____

Word Box

afraid	broken	cedar	sofa	asleep
gerbil	ribbon	carpet	alike	awake
around	water	carrot	lesson	under

Writing sentences with words that have the schwa sound

Name _____

Syllables

Divide each word into syllables.
Then write the number of syllables you count.

1. **work•book**
   _2_ syllables

2. **rabbit**
   ____ syllables

3. **star**
   ____ syllables

4. **telephone**
   ____ syllables

5. **trumpet**
   ____ syllables

6. **daffodil**
   ____ syllables

7. **poodle**
   ____ syllables

8. **potato**
   ____ syllables

9. **caterpillar**
   ____ syllables

10. **frost**
    ____ syllables

Name _____

Read Aloud

 The vowel in an unstressed syllable will usually have the /u/ sound. This is called the **schwa** sound and is marked as ə.

Read aloud each pair of words.
Circle the word that contains the **schwa** sound.

1. (dragon)   volcano   8. gallop   trot

2. heavy   model   9. even   smooth

3. oboe   again   10. earth   pasta

4. brain   minute   11. label   tape

5. angel   flute   12. jacket   picnic

6. tuna   many   13. puppy   chicken

7. grizzly   panda   14. cookie   lemon

Review: Syllables and schwa

Prefixes & Suffixes

Basic Phonics Skills, Level D • EMC 3321 • ©2004 by Evan-Moor Corp.

Name _____

Prefix **dis**

A **prefix** is added to the beginning of a word.
It changes the meaning of the word.
   dis—not; the opposite of
      I **like** apples.
      I **dislike** squash.

Add the prefix **dis** to the words.
Then match the new words to their meaning.

_____honest   put an end to; stopped

_____armed   not truthful

_____continued   to take away someone's hopes

_____agreement   a loss or lack of skills

_____like   having no weapon

_____courage   to have a feeling against something

_____ability   a difference of opinion

Fill in the missing words.

1. The police officer _____ the robber.

2. The store _____ products that did not sell.

3. She had a _____ with her best friend.

4. I _____ eating liver and onions for dinner.

5. The man's _____ keeps him in a wheelchair.

Writing words with the prefix dis

Name _____

Prefix re

A **prefix** is added to the beginning of a word.
It changes the meaning of the word.
  re—again
    I **folded** the napkins before dinner.
    I have to **refold** them after they are washed.

Add the prefix **re** to the words.
Then match the new words to their meaning.

____re____wrap - - - - - - - - - - - - - - - - to cover in something again

_____write   to find again

_____paint   to build again

_____turn   to put something on again

_____apply   to copy over again

_____build   to paint again

_____discover   to come back again

Fill in the missing words.

1. I tore the paper on the gift, so I had to _____ it.

2. My homework was messy, so I had to _____ it.

3. Ted likes to _____ the fence every year.

4. When will he _____ from vacation?

5. They had to _____ the barn after the fire.

Writing words with the prefix **re**

Basic Phonics Skills, Level D • EMC 3321 • ©2004 by Evan-Moor Corp.

Name _____

Prefix **un**

A **prefix** is added to the beginning of a word.
It changes the meaning of the word.
un—not; the opposite of
I was **sure** I could read the book.
I was **unsure** that I could pass the test.

Add the prefix **un** to the words.
Then match the new words to their meaning.

____un____wrap   not ready to be eaten

_____happy   to remove paper from something

_____known   to feel sad

_____ripe   cannot do something

_____able   something that is not needed

_____kind   something that is not known

_____necessary   not a kind person

Fill in the missing words.

1. Mattie wants to _____ her birthday present.

2. Don't eat _____ fruit or you may get an
upset stomach.

3. He was _____ when his best friend moved away.

4. Tim was _____ to finish his homework last night.

5. It is _____ to go to school on Saturday.

Writing words with the prefix **un**

Name _____

Circle the prefix in each word.

1. unknown

2. disagree

3. reapply

4. discourage

5. unsure

6. rebuild

7. discover

8. unfriendly

9. rerun

10. untangle

11. return

12. discontinue

Write one sentence using both words.

1. unable	rebuild

2. unfriendly	disagree

3. discover	unknown

Reading words with prefixes

Name _____

Suffix ful

A **suffix** is added to the end of a word.
It changes the meaning of the word.
ful—full of
I am **hopeful** that I will win the race.

Add the suffix **ful** to the words.
Then match the new words to their meaning.

wonder___ful___ - - - - - - - - - - unusually good; filled with wonder

care_____   not clumsy or awkward

thought_____   afraid; not brave

grace_____   useful to others

fear_____   give close attention to; being cautious

help_____   showing great happiness

joy_____   considerate

Fill in the missing words.

1. The ballet dancer was very _____.

2. The girl was _____ of spiders.

3. Be _____ when you cross the street!

4. Please be _____ and clean up this mess.

5. Morris had a _____ surprise on his birthday.

Writing words with the suffix **ful**

Name _____

Suffix less

Phonics Fact!

A **suffix** is added to the end of a word.
It changes the meaning of the word.
less—without
The newborn kitten was **helpless**.

Add the suffix **less** to the words.
Then match the new words to their meaning.

thought__less__ - - - - - - - - - - careless; inconsiderate of others

hope_____   not dangerous

care_____   unable to help yourself

use_____   brave

help_____   done without paying close attention

fear_____   without a use

harm_____   without hope

Fill in the missing words.

1. A garden snake is _____ to people.

2. It was _____ of Megan to forget her
friend's birthday.

3. The _____ firefighter rescued the boy from
the burning building.

4. A broken lamp is _____ at night.

5. Don't make a _____ mistake on the test.

Writing words with the suffix **less**

Name _____

Suffix ly

A **suffix** is added to the end of a word.
It changes the meaning of the word.
ly—in a certain manner
She **carefully** picked up the frightened kitten.

Add the suffix **ly** to the words.
In some words, you must change the final **y** to **i** and then add the suffix.
Match the new words to their meaning.

busy_____ily_____   in a fast way

kind_____   working without stopping

quiet_____   impatiently; with great desire

merry_____   unhappily

quick_____   without any noise

eager_____   in a gentle or thoughtful manner

sad_____   filled with fun and laughter

Fill in the missing words.

1. Sara _____ opened the letter from her
   grandmother.

2. The boys played _____ while the baby took a nap.

3. Hank _____ worked on the test questions in
   order to finish on time.

4. Amy _____ told her teacher that she had
   lost her lunch money.

5. The twins _____ skipped down the trail.

Writing words with the suffix **ly**

Name _____

Find the Suffixes

Circle the prefix in each word.

1. harmless   7. kindly

2. useful   8. hopeful

3. quickly   9. fearless

4. helpless   10. restless

5. graceful   11. happily

6. softly   12. wonderful

Write one sentence using both words.

1. wonderful   kindly
_____
_____
2. fearless   harmful
_____
_____
3. useful   helpless
_____
_____

Reading words with suffixes

 Basic Phonics Skills, Level D • EMC 3321 • ©2004 by Evan-Moor Corp.

Name _____

Prefix or Suffix?

Add a prefix or a suffix to the word to complete the sentences.

Prefixes	Suffixes
dis	less
un	ful
re	ly

1. The ballgame was _____ when it started to rain.
   continued

2. When will Father _____ from his business trip?
   turn

3. The ballet dancer _____ leaped into the air.
   graceful

4. Black widow spiders can be _____ to people.
   harm

5. My dog chewed on my story, so I had to _____ it.
   write

6. My little brother _____ getting his hair cut.
   likes

7. He was _____ when he lost his watch.
   happy

8. The _____ bear protected her cubs from the
   fear
   hungry wolves.

Deciding when to use a suffix or a prefix

Plural and Inflectional Endings

Basic Phonics Skills, Level D • EMC 3321 • ©2004 by Evan-Moor Corp.

Name _____

Plural Words

- The word **singular** means "only one."
- The word **plural** means "more than one."
- To make a word plural, you usually add **-s** (**cat/cats**).
- For words that end in the letters **s**, **ch**, **sh**, **ss**, and **x**, add **-es** (**buses**, **inches**, **classes**, **boxes**).

Make each word plural by adding **-s** or **-es**.
Write the word on the line.

1. plane

planes

2. dress

_____

3. fox

_____

4. patch

_____

5. stamp

_____

6. dish

_____

7. bike

_____

8. bus

_____

9. glass

_____

Plural endings: Adding **-s** or **-es**

Name _____

One . . . Two . . .

- When a word ends with a <u>consonant</u> and **y**, change the **y** to **i** and add **-es**.

    baby   **babies**

- When a word ends with a <u>vowel</u> and **y**, just add **-s**.

    key   **keys**

Write the plural form of each word.

1.  One berry   Two _____

2.  One pony   Two _____

3.  One candy   Two _____

4. One cherry   Two _____

5. One fairy   Two _____

6. One lady   Two _____

7. One monkey   Two _____

8. One boy   Two _____

9. One fly   Two _____

10. One daisy   Two _____

Plural endings: Changing y to i and add -es

Name _____

See the Puppies?

- When a word ends with a <u>consonant</u> and **y**, change the **y** to **i** and add **-es**.
    baby   **babies**
- When a word ends with a <u>vowel</u> and **y**, just add **-s**.
    key   **keys**

Write the plural form of the word to complete each sentence.

1. Janet saw six cute _____ at the shelter.   **puppy**

2. Clare was invited to two birthday _____.   **party**

3. Dan gave her ten _____ for a dime.   **penny**

4. _____ are beautiful insects.   **Butterfly**

5. Sue watched both _____ for her sister.   **baby**

6. My vacation is going to be ten _____ long.   **day**

7. Bob kept shooing _____ away from his food.   **fly**

8. Little Billy wanted to play with all of the _____.   **toy**

9. New York and Boston are two big _____.   **city**

10. "Cinderella" is one of my favorite _____.   **story**

Plural endings: Changing y to i and add -es

Name _____

Look at the Leaves!

Singular	Plural	Singular	Plural
1. calf	calves	6. loaf	
2. elf		7. leaf	
3. half		8. shelf	
4. knife		9. wife	
5. life		10. wolf	

Write the plural form of the underlined word.

1. Do you have a <u>calf</u>?

I have five _____.

2. Is there a red <u>leaf</u> on the tree?

There are many red _____ on the tree.

3. Did you buy one <u>loaf</u> of bread?

No, I bought three _____ of bread.

Plural endings: Changing f/fe to v and add -es

Name _____

Lots of Things

Some singular words change their spelling when they are made plural.

man   **men**

Draw lines to match the singular and plural forms.

mouse   feet

woman   geese

goose   mice

foot   women

person   teeth

child   oxen

ox   children

tooth   people

Circle the word that completes the sentence.

1. The _____ wants to go to the zoo.

child   **children**

2. How many _____ did the dentist pull?

tooth   **teeth**

3. That _____ is wearing a funny hat.

woman   **women**

4. Do _____ have webbed feet?

goose   **geese**

Irregular plural endings

Name _____

Making Plurals

Read each singular word.
Write its plural form in the correct box.

Add **-s**	Add **-es**
Change y to i and add -es	**Change f/fe to v and add -es**

Word Box

baby	half	pencil	elf	dish
pen	plane	penny	brush	flower
berry	story	kiss	wolf	calf
leaf	fox	inch	fly	class
pass	puppy	knife	city	shoe

Review: Plural endings

Name _____

Adding -ing
Part 1

Adding **-ing** to a verb tells that an action is ongoing.
- When a verb ends with two or more consonants, just add **-ing**.
  walk   walking   fight   fighting
- When a verb ends in a consonant and an **e**, remove the **e** before adding **-ing**.
  ride   riding   believe   believing

Read each sentence.
Add **-ing** to the word to complete the sentence.

1. You're always ___talking___ on the phone!   **talk**

2. Althea is _____ in the other room.   **sleep**

3. We are _____ some cookies now.   **make**

4. Who is _____ on my door?   **knock**

5. Lloyd is supposed to be _____ the leaves.   **rake**

6. My sister and I are _____ in a recital.   **dance**

7. Stop _____ on the bed!   **jump**

8. We enjoy _____ the ball at recess.   **kick**

9. The light is _____ in my eyes.   **shine**

10. My parents are _____ in the election tomorrow.   **vote**

Name _____

Adding -ing
Part 2

 **Phonics Fact!**

When a verb ends with one short vowel and one consonant, double the final consonant before adding **-ing**. The double consonant keeps the vowel short.

sit	sitting	stop stopping

Circle each word that ends with one short vowel and one consonant. Add **-ing** to those words only.

1. (hop) _hopping_

2. spend _____

3. skip _____

4. tap _____

5. camp _____

6. drag _____

7. nap _____

8. drip _____

Choose one of the **-ing** words to complete each sentence.

1. The kangaroo is _____ away!

2. The kindergarteners are still _____.

3. Bob is always _____ his pencil on his desk.

4. The girls enjoy _____ down the hallway.

Adding **-ing**

Basic Phonics Skills, Level D • EMC 3321 • ©2004 by Evan-Moor Corp.

Name _____

Tried and True

Phonics Fact!

- To add the ending **-ed** to a verb that ends in a consonant and **y**, change the **y** to **i** and add **-ed**.

  try   **tried**

- If you want to add **-ing** to a verb that ends in a consonant and **y**, keep the **y** and add **-ing**.

  try   **trying**

Add **-ed** to each verb and write it on the first line.
Then add **-ing** and write it on the second line.

1. cry  *cried* _____ *crying* _____	**2.** fry  _____ _____	**3.** dry  _____ _____
4. spy  _____ _____	**5.** pry  _____ _____	**6.** worry  _____ _____

Inflectional endings: Words ending in y

Name _____

Playing with Words

Phonics Fact!

- If a verb ends in a <u>vowel</u> and **y**, do not change the **y**. Just add **-ed** or **-ing**.

  | play | played | playing |

- If a verb ends in a <u>consonant</u> and **y**, change the **y** to **i** and add **-ed**. To add **-ing**, keep the **y**.

  | dry | dried | drying |

Add the endings to each verb.

	Add -ed	**Add -ing**
1. marry	_____	_____
2. spray	_____	_____
3. cry	_____	_____
4. carry	_____	_____
5. try	_____	_____
6. play	_____	_____
7. hurry	_____	_____
8. enjoy	_____	_____
9. spy	_____	_____
10. pray	_____	_____
11. rely	_____	_____
12. stay	_____	_____

Inflectional endings: Words ending in y

Basic Phonics Skills, Level D • EMC 3321 • ©2004 by Evan-Moor Corp.

Take It Slowly

Phonics Fact!

- Adding the ending **-ly** to an adjective usually changes it into an adverb. An adverb tells when, where, how, or how much. Most words that end in **-ly** are adverbs.

  slow   **slowly**

- If the base word ends in **y,** change the **y** to **i** and add **-ly.**

  happy   **happily**

Read each sentence.
Change the underlined word from an adjective to an adverb.
Add **-ly**. Write the adverb on the line.

1. Bernie is a <u>quick</u> worker.

He works _____quickly_____.

2. Martha is so <u>brave</u>.

She behaves _____.

3. The <u>loud</u> fans cheered.

They yelled _____.

4. I was so <u>busy</u> yesterday.

I _____ did all of my chores.

5. Ms. Mir is <u>happy</u> to help.

She _____ helps her students.

6. The toddler was <u>angry</u>.

He _____ threw his toys on the floor.

Inflectional endings: Adding **-ly**

Name _____

Which Ending?

Read each sentence.
Add the correct ending to each word.
Write the word on the line.

1. The teacher told Lisa and me to stop ____talking____ so
   much in class.
   talk

2. The three rabbits hopped _____ all over our
   backyard.
   happy

3. My little sister _____ in her crib this morning.
   nap

4. We are _____ in the ballet on Sunday.
   dance

5. My brother _____ chocolate chip cookies
   last night.
   bake

6. The team has _____ hard for the big game.
   practice

7. Greg's kickstand keeps _____ on the ground.
   drag

8. The cheerleaders are _____ because our
   team won!
   jump

9. Marie _____ her foot to the beat of the song.
   tap

10. Beverly is _____ decorations for the party.
    make

Review: Inflectional endings

Word Family Practice

How to Use:

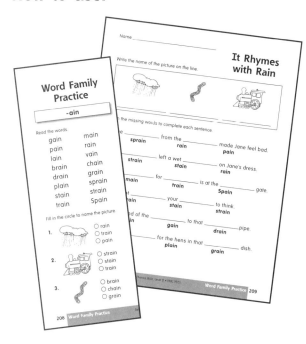

After students practice the words on the Word Family Practice strip, follow up with the sentence completion activity.

Word Family Practice

-ain	

Read the words.

gain	main
pain	rain
lain	vain
brain	chain
drain	grain
plain	sprain
stain	strain
train	Spain

Fill in the circle to name the picture.

1.
   ○ rain
   ○ train
   ○ pain

2.
   ○ strain
   ○ stain
   ○ train

3.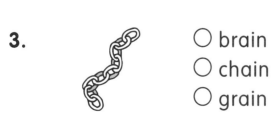
   ○ brain
   ○ chain
   ○ grain

Word Family Practice

-aw	

Read the words.

caw	jaw
law	paw
raw	saw
claw	thaw
draw	flaw
slaw	straw
gnaw	Shaw

Fill in the circle to name the picture.

1. ○ paw
   ○ claw
   ○ jaw

2. ○ raw
   ○ law
   ○ gnaw

3. ○ saw
   ○ slaw
   ○ straw

    Basic Phonics Skills, Level D • EMC 3321 • ©2004 by Evan-Moor Corp.

Name _____

It Rhymes with Rain

Write the name of the picture on the line.

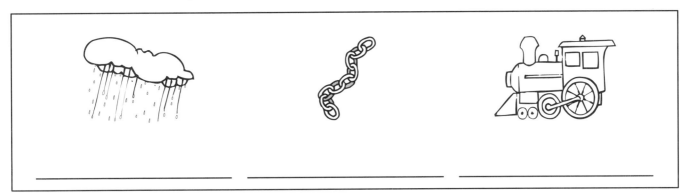

_____   _____   _____

Fill in the missing words to complete each sentence.

1. The _____ from the _____ made Jane feel bad.
        sprain   **rain**   **pain**

2. The _____ left a wet _____ on Jane's dress.
        strain   **stain**   **rain**

3. The _____ for _____ is at the _____ gate.
        main   **train**   **Spain**

4. It will not _____ your _____ to think.
        brain   **stain**   **strain**

5. Link the end of the _____ to that _____ pipe.
        chain   **gain**   **drain**

6. Put the _____ for the hens in that _____ dish.
        gain   **plain**   **grain**

Name _____

It Rhymes with Paw

Write the name of the picture on the line.

_____   _____   _____

Fill in the missing word or words to complete each sentence.

1. The crow grabbed _____ in its _____.
   claw   **straw**   **raw**

2. _____ likes to _____ his pet dog.
   Shaw   **thaw**   **draw**

3. A kitten's _____ has four very sharp _____.
   paw   **claws**   **jaw**

4. Mom used _____ cabbage to make cole_____
   for dinner.
   jaw   **raw**   **slaw**

5. The shark opened its _____ to _____ on its meal.
   gnaw   **jaws**   **caws**

6. As we watched the ice _____, we _____ some
   ice crystals.
   saw   **law**   **thaw**

Basic Phonics Skills, Level D • EMC 3321 • ©2004 by Evan-Moor Corp.

Word Family Practice

-are

Read the words.

bare	care
dare	fare
hare	mare
pare	rare
blare	flare
glare	scare
share	snare
spare	square
stare	compare

Fill in the circle to name the picture.

1.
   - ○ pare
   - ○ mare
   - ○ bare

2.
   - ○ stare
   - ○ spare
   - ○ scare

3.
   - ○ square
   - ○ snare
   - ○ share

Word Family Practice

-air

Read the words.

air	fair
hair	lair
pair	chair
flair	stairs
repair	despair
unfair	

Fill in the circle to name the picture.

1.
   - ○ flair
   - ○ fare
   - ○ chair

2.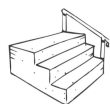
   - ○ unfair
   - ○ stairs
   - ○ pair

3.
   - ○ repair
   - ○ unfair
   - ○ pair

Name _____

Write the name of the picture on the line.

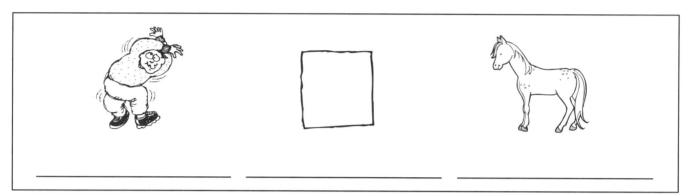

_____   _____   _____

Fill in the missing word or words to complete each sentence.

1. What is the train _____ to New York City?
       pare   **dare**   **fare**

2. Do you like a pizza to be _____ or round?
       ware   **square**   **spare**

3. Dan, please _____ a turtle and a _____ for the class.
       hare   **compare**   **flare**

4. Would you _____ to take _____ of my pet snake?
       dare   **fare**   **care**

5. The _____ from that light will _____ the

_____.
       mare   **glare**   **scare**

6. The hunter caught a _____ in his _____.
       care   **snare**   **hare**

       Basic Phonics Skills, Level D • EMC 3321 • ©2004 by Evan-Moor Corp.

Name _____

It Rhymes with Air

Write the name of the picture on the line.

_____   _____   _____

Fill in the missing word or words to complete each sentence.

1. It is better not to run on the _____.

        chair   **stairs**   **fair**

2. How much _____ does it take to fill a balloon?

        fair   **hair**   **air**

3. George felt it was _____ that his sister got to go to

the _____ and he did not.

        unfair   **despair**   **fair**

4. My cat always leaves _____ all over the _____.

        pair   **chair**   **hair**

5. A _____ of foxes ran into their _____ to escape
the hunter.

        pair   **lair**   **fair**

6. Don't _____. I can _____ your bike.

        repair   **despair**   **unfair**

Word Family Practice

-ew

Read the words.

dew	few
new	pew
yew	brew
blew	crew
chew	flew
drew	screw
knew	stew
slew	threw

Fill in the circle to name the picture.

1.
   ○ dew
   ○ blew
   ○ drew

2.
   ○ drew
   ○ brew
   ○ dew

3.
   ○ crew
   ○ stew
   ○ chew

Word Family Practice

-ead

Read the words.

dead	head
lead	read
bread	dread
spread	thread
tread	

Fill in the circle to name the picture.

1.
   ○ dead
   ○ bread
   ○ dread

2.
   ○ thread
   ○ tread
   ○ lead

3.
   ○ read
   ○ thread
   ○ head

 Basic Phonics Skills, Level D • EMC 3321 • ©2004 by Evan-Moor Corp.

Name _____

It Rhymes with New

Write the name of the picture on the line.

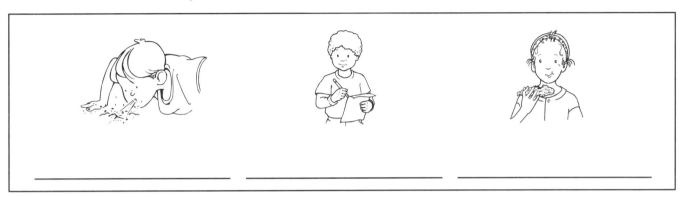

_____   _____   _____

Fill in the missing words to complete each sentence.

1. A _____ gulls _____ over the beach.
        blew   **flew**   **few**

2. The _____ _____ came aboard the ship last night.
        chew   **new**   **crew**

3. Be sure to _____ the meat in the _____.
        stew   **chew**   **screw**

4. Bob _____ his kite up into the air and the wind

_____ it away.
        blew   **knew**   **threw**

5. I _____ that the grass would be wet with _____
this morning.
        few   **dew**   **knew**

6. Would you please _____ some tea for the thirsty

_____?
        crew   **blew**   **brew**

Name _____

It Rhymes with Head

Write the name of the picture on the line.

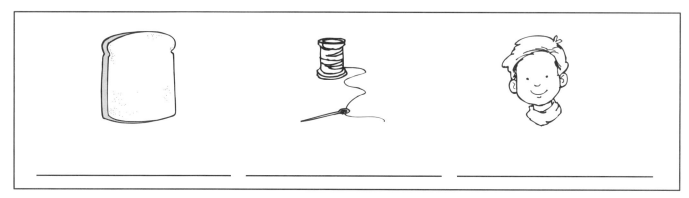

_____   _____   _____

Fill in the missing word or words to complete each sentence.

1. How thick is the _____ on the tire?

        dead   **thread**   **tread**

2. The _____ in my pencil is almost gone.

        head   **lead**   **read**

3. Mike _____ to his little sister every day.

        spread   **read**   **lead**

4. I always _____ going to the dentist.

        dread   **lead**   **thread**

5. Ann likes to _____ jam on her _____.

        dread   **bread**   **spread**

6. We found a _____ flea on our dog's _____.

        head   **dead**   **read**

Basic Phonics Skills, Level D • EMC 3321 • ©2004 by Evan-Moor Corp.

Word Family Practice

-eak

Read the words.

beak	leak
peak	teak
weak	bleak
creak	sneak
speak	squeak
streak	

Fill in the circle to name the picture.

1.
   - ○ teak
   - ○ beak
   - ○ peak

2.
   - ○ sneak
   - ○ speak
   - ○ squeak

3.
   - ○ bleak
   - ○ teak
   - ○ leak

Word Family Practice

-eed

Read the words.

deed	feed
heed	need
reed	seed
weed	bleed
breed	creed
freed	greed
speed	steed

Fill in the circle to name the picture.

1.
   - ○ weed
   - ○ reed
   - ○ seed

2.
   - ○ bleed
   - ○ freed
   - ○ feed

3.
   - ○ speed
   - ○ steed
   - ○ seed

Name _____

Write the name of the picture on the line.

_____   _____   _____

Fill in the missing word or words to complete each sentence.

1. It's hard to _____ if the floors _____.
          peak   **creak**   **sneak**

2. The hungry little mouse began to _____.
          squeak   **bleak**   **streak**

3. It was hard to see the mountain _____ on the

    _____ morning.
        bleak   **weak**   **peak**

4. The owl used its sharp _____ to eat its food.
        leak   **bleak**   **beak**

5. Will the roof _____ when it rains?
       speak   **leak**   **teak**

6. The sick man was too _____ to _____.
       weak   **speak**   **creak**

Name _____

It Rhymes
with Seed

Write the name of the picture on the line.

_____   _____   _____

Fill in the missing word or words to complete each sentence.

1. Pull the _____, and then plant the _____.

        speed   **seeds**   **weeds**

2. The black _____ was famous for its _____.

        steed   **speed**   **greed**

3. Amos _____ the duck caught in the _____.

        reeds   **freed**   **bleed**

4. You _____ to _____ the rules when you play
a game.

        need   **feed**   **heed**

5. Do you ever _____ _____ to the wild birds?

        creed   **feed**   **seeds**

6. The knight did a brave _____.

        deed   **breed**   **freed**

Word Family Practice

-oy

Read the words.

boy	coy
joy	soy
toy	Roy
Troy	ploy
employ	enjoy
destroy	

Fill in the circle to name the picture.

1.
- ○ joy
- ○ toy
- ○ boy

2.
- ○ joy
- ○ toy
- ○ coy

3.
- ○ employ
- ○ ploy
- ○ enjoy

Word Family Practice

-oil

Read the words.

oil	boil
coil	foil
toil	soil
spoil	broil

Fill in the circle to name the picture.

1.
- ○ foil
- ○ soil
- ○ boil

2.
- ○ coil
- ○ oil
- ○ toil

3.
- ○ spoil
- ○ coil
- ○ soil

 Basic Phonics Skills, Level D • EMC 3321 • ©2004 by Evan-Moor Corp.

Name _____

Write the name of the picture on the line.

_____   _____   _____

Fill in the missing word or words to complete each sentence.

1. Is the new baby a _____ or a girl?
    soy   **coy**   **boy**

2. _____ and _____ are twin boys.
    Roy   **Joy**   **Troy**

3. I don't like the taste of _____ milk.
    toy   **soy**   **ploy**

4. Playing with the new _____ filled the girl with

_____.
    joy   **coy**   **toy**

5. What tool will they use to _____ that old building?
    destroy   **soy**   **enjoy**

6. What _____ did he use to trick his friend?
    soy   **ploy**   **toy**

Name _____

It Rhymes with Boil

Write the name of the picture on the line.

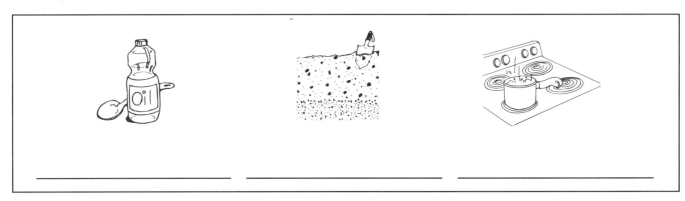

_____   _____   _____

Fill in the missing word or words to complete each sentence.

1. You must turn the _____ over before planting seeds.
        coil   **soil**   **spoil**

2. Milk will _____ if you don't keep it in the refrigerator.
      soil   **foil**   **spoil**

3. Please stack that _____ of wire on a shelf in the garage.
      toil   **coil**   **foil**

4. Did you cover the dish with _____ before you put it away?
      foil   **coil**   **soil**

5. Will the chef _____ or _____ the meat?
      spoil   **boil**   **broil**

6. I would rub olive _____ on the meat and put it in the

oven to _____.
      broil   **foil**   **oil**

 Basic Phonics Skills, Level D • EMC 3321 • ©2004 by Evan-Moor Corp.

Word Family Practice

-udge

Read the words.

budge   fudge

judge   nudge

drudge   grudge

sludge   smudge

trudge

Fill in the circle to name the picture.

1.
   - ○ drudge
   - ○ grudge
   - ○ fudge

2.
   - ○ budge
   - ○ judge
   - ○ trudge

3.
   - ○ nudge
   - ○ sludge
   - ○ trudge

Word Family Practice

-ight

Read the words.

fight   light

might   tight

right   sight

night   knight

blight   bright

flight   fright

plight   slight

Fill in the circle to name the picture.

1.
   - ○ a knight in a fight
   - ○ a bright light
   - ○ a dark night

2.
   - ○ a knight in a fight
   - ○ a bright light
   - ○ a dark night

3.
   - ○ a knight in a fight
   - ○ a bright light
   - ○ a dark night

Name _____

It Rhymes with Fudge

Write the name of the picture on the line.

_____   _____   _____

Fill in the missing word or words to complete each sentence.

1. Will you be the _____ of the contest?

       budge   **judge**   **trudge**

2. The boy had a _____ against his nextdoor neighbor.

       nudge   **sludge**   **grudge**

3. We had to _____ through the snow to get from the car to the house.

       budge   **trudge**   **grudge**

4. You should clean any _____ out of the rain gutters.

       sludge   **budge**   **judge**

5. My car won't _____. Will you please give it

  a _____?

       smudge   **budge**   **nudge**

6. Sam got a _____ of _____ on his homework paper.

       fudge   **budge**   **smudge**

Basic Phonics Skills, Level D • EMC 3321 • ©2004 by Evan-Moor Corp.

Name _____

It Rhymes with Light

Write the name of the picture on the line.

_____   _____   _____

Fill in the missing words to complete each sentence.

1. Tim saw a _____ _____ last _____.
        night   **bright**   **light**

2. Is it _____ to get into a _____?
        might   **fight**   **right**

3. The plane _____ will start _____ here.
        flight   **right**   **fright**

4. The _____ got a _____ when he saw the dragon.
        fright   **knight**   **fight**

5. We _____ have to turn on a _____.
        light   **flight**   **might**

6. Be sure to buy the _____ size shoes. They should not be

too _____.
        slight   **tight**   **right**

Word Family Practice

-oop

Read the words.

coop	hoop
loop	droop
scoop	sloop
snoop	stoop
swoop	troop
whoop	

Fill in the circle to name the picture.

1.
   ○ loop
   ○ hoop
   ○ droop

2.
   ○ snoop
   ○ swoop
   ○ scoop

3.
   ○ coop
   ○ scoop
   ○ snoop

Word Family Practice

-ook

Read the words.

book	cook
hook	look
nook	rook
took	brook
crook	shook

Fill in the circle to name the picture.

1.
   ○ book
   ○ hook
   ○ took

2.
   ○ look
   ○ hook
   ○ nook

3.
   ○ shook
   ○ cook
   ○ brook

 Basic Phonics Skills, Level D • EMC 3321 • ©2004 by Evan-Moor Corp.

Name _____

It Rhymes with Hoop

Write the name of the picture on the line.

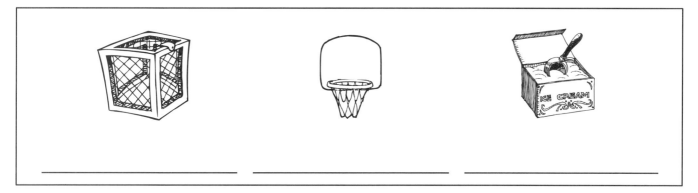

_____   _____   _____

Fill in the missing word or words to complete each sentence.

1. It isn't nice to _____ .

           troop   **hoop**   **snoop**

2. Will you help me clean up the chicken _____?

           loop   **coop**   **sloop**

3. A hawk will often _____ down and _____ up
a mouse.

           scoop   **swoop**   **snoop**

4. "Don't _____ when you stand," the general told

his _____ .

           troops   **scoop**   **droop**

5. Quick! Toss the basketball into the _____!

           hoop   **sloop**   **loop**

6. The _____ quickly sailed across the bay.

           scoop   **sloop**   **loop**

©2004 by Evan-Moor Corp. • Basic Phonics Skills, Level D • EMC 3321**Word Family Practice** 227

Name _____

It Rhymes with Book

Write the name of the picture on the line.

_____   _____   _____

Fill in the missing word or words to complete each sentence.

1. Help! A _____ _____ my car!
      shook   **took**   **crook**

2. Please hang your coat on that _____.
      rook   **look**   **hook**

3. Dad uses the _____ _____ all the time.
      book   **cook**   **rook**

4. Lee _____ his piggy bank to empty it.
      brook   **shook**   **cook**

5. You may see polliwogs when you _____ in

the _____.
      brook   **hook**   **look**

6. Sally found a cozy _____ where she could sit and

read her _____.
      book   **look**   **nook**

Basic Phonics Skills, Level D • EMC 3321 • ©2004 by Evan-Moor Corp.

Word Family Practice

-ow (long o)

Read the words.

bow	low
mow	row
sow	tow
know	blow
flow	glow
show	slow
snow	stow

Fill in the circle to name the picture.

1.
   ○ blow
   ○ flow
   ○ bow

2.
   ○ row
   ○ sow
   ○ mow

3.
   ○ sow
   ○ snow
   ○ show

Word Family Practice

-ow

Read the words.

bow	cow
how	now
vow	sow
wow	brow
chow	plow

Fill in the circle to name the picture.

1.
   ○ sow
   ○ cow
   ○ vow

2.
   ○ cow
   ○ chow
   ○ sow

3.
   ○ wow
   ○ plow
   ○ now

Name _____

It Rhymes with Snow

Write the name of the picture on the line.

_____   _____   _____

Fill in the missing word or words to complete each sentence.

1. Can you _____ me how to tie a _____?
　　　　glow　　　　　　**show**　　　　　　　**bow**

2. The wind began to _____ the _____flakes around.
　　　　snow　　　　　　**blow**　　　　　　**show**

3. I _____ how to _____ seeds in a _____.
　　　row　　　　　　**know**　　　　　　**sow**

4. The tortoise was _____, but he won the race.
　　　low　　　　　　**blow**　　　　　　**slow**

5. After you _____ the grass, _____ the lawn
　　　mower in the shed.
　　　stow　　　　　　**grow**　　　　　　**mow**

6. The _____ of the campfire was pretty.
　　　grow　　　　　　**glow**　　　　　　**flow**

 Basic Phonics Skills, Level D • EMC 3321 • ©2004 by Evan-Moor Corp.

Name _____

Write the name of the picture on the line.

_____   _____   _____

Fill in the missing word or words to complete each sentence.

1. _____ much grain should I give the _____?
           chow   **How**   **cow**

2. Should I _____ the fields _____ or later?
         now   **plow**   **brow**

3. The man must _____ to the queen.
         plow   **bow**   **chow**

4. The mother _____ had six piglets.
         cow   **bow**   **sow**

5. A _____ is a promise you must keep.
         wow   **vow**   **now**

6. The carpenter worked so hard that he had sweat on

his _____.
         chow   **plow**   **brow**

Word Family Practice

-out

Read the words.

out	bout
gout	pout
grout	shout
scout	spout
snout	stout
sprout	about
trout	

Fill in the circle to name the picture.

1.
   - ○ scout
   - ○ snout
   - ○ trout

2.
   - ○ shout
   - ○ stout
   - ○ trout

3.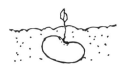
   - ○ spout
   - ○ snout
   - ○ sprout

Word Family Practice

-ound

Read the words.

bound	found
hound	mound
pound	round
sound	wound
ground	around

Fill in the circle to name the picture.

1.
   - ○ pound
   - ○ round
   - ○ hound

2.
   - ○ ground
   - ○ wound
   - ○ found

3. ○
   - ○ sound
   - ○ round
   - ○ bound

   Basic Phonics Skills, Level D • EMC 3321 • ©2004 by Evan-Moor Corp.

Name _____

It Rhymes with Out

Write the name of the picture on the line.

_____   _____   _____

Fill in the missing word or words to complete each sentence.

1. Do you think my seeds will begin to _____ soon?

          shout   **snout**   **sprout**

2. The camper tossed a _____ to the bear cub and hit

  its _____.

          trout   **snout**   **spout**

3. Don't _____ because you didn't catch a _____.

          bout   **trout**   **pout**

4. Please go _____side if you are going to _____.

          bout   **shout**   **out**

5. I read a story _____ a Boy _____ who camped in
  the woods.

          bout   **about**   **Scout**

6. That _____ old man had _____ in his foot.

          sprout   **stout**   **gout**

Name _____

It Rhymes with Hound

Write the name of the picture on the line.

_____   _____   _____

Fill in the missing word or words to complete each sentence.

1. Kim _____ the ribbon _____ the gift box.
    found   **around**   **wound**

2. Pete _____ his _____ rolling on a _____ of dirt.
    hound   **found**   **mound**

3. Please help me _____ this pole into the _____.
    pound   **ground**   **round**

4. What a _____ that boy made when he fell down!
    bound   **sound**   **wound**

5. Is a ball _____ or flat?
    mound   **round**   **hound**

6. I _____ a pretty rock on the play_____.
    ground   **bound**   **found**

Basic Phonics Skills, Level D • EMC 3321 • ©2004 by Evan-Moor Corp.

Word Family Practice

-ark

Read the words.

bark	dark
hark	lark
mark	park
shark	spark
stark	Clark

Fill in the circle to name the picture.

1.
   - ○ stark
   - ○ spark
   - ○ shark

2.
   - ○ hark
   - ○ lark
   - ○ dark

3.
   - ○ mark
   - ○ bark
   - ○ park

Word Family Practice

-ore

Read the words.

bore	core
fore	gore
more	lore
sore	pore
wore	tore
score	chore
snore	shore
store	spore
before	swore

Fill in the circle to name the picture.

1.
   - ○ store
   - ○ spore
   - ○ shore

2.
   - ○ chore
   - ○ shore
   - ○ sore

3.
   - ○ chore
   - ○ tore
   - ○ score

Name _____

Write the name of the picture on the line.

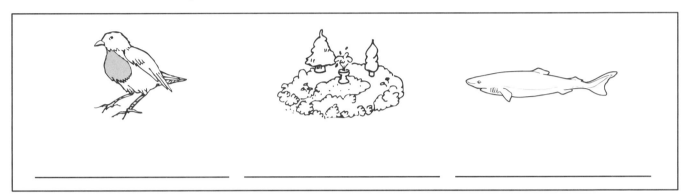

_____   _____   _____

Fill in the missing word or words to complete each sentence.

1. Did you hear that dog _____ last night?
       park   **bark**   **dark**

2. Where did you _____ the car?
       bark   **mark**   **park**

3. A huge _____ swam near our boat.
       lark   **shark**   **spark**

4. Did you _____ the map to show how to get to

the _____?
       mark   **park**   **spark**

5. I saw a _____ of lightning in the _____ sky.
       dark   **mark**   **spark**

6. The poem read "_____! I hear a _____ singing."
       park   **Hark**   **lark**

 Basic Phonics Skills, Level D • EMC 3321 • ©2004 by Evan-Moor Corp.

Name _____

Write the name of the picture on the line.

Yammy Bakery

_____   _____   _____

Fill in the missing word or words to complete each sentence.

1. You can hear Dad _____ all through the house!
     more   **snore**   **shore**

2. Can we _____ _____ than their team?
     more   **fore**   **score**

3. He _____ a bandage on his _____ knee.
     sore   **wore**   **pore**

4. The golfer shouted, "_____!" and then hit the ball.
     swore   **score**   **Fore**

5. Cut out the _____ of the apple _____ you bake it.
     core   **before**   **store**

6. There was _____ _____ in that movie than

I have ever seen _____!
     more   **before**   **gore**

Little Phonics Readers

BASIC Phonics Skills

What Jack Saw

-ack family

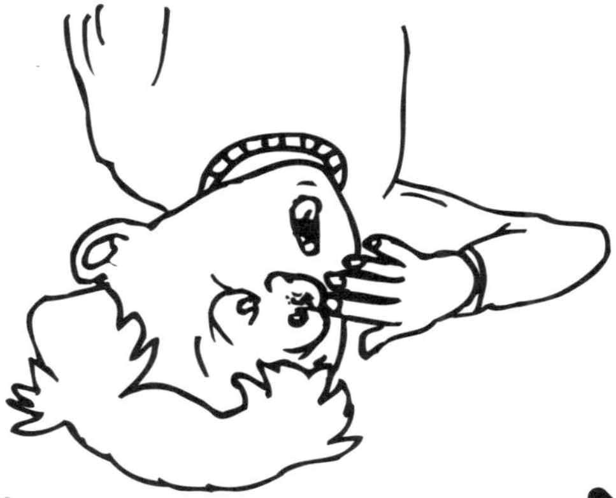

There was an old shack in back of the barn.

When Jack went into the shack, he saw a stack of sacks.

The sack on top of the stack wiggled. A "Quack, quack" came from the sack.

1

fold 2

fold 1

6

Think About It

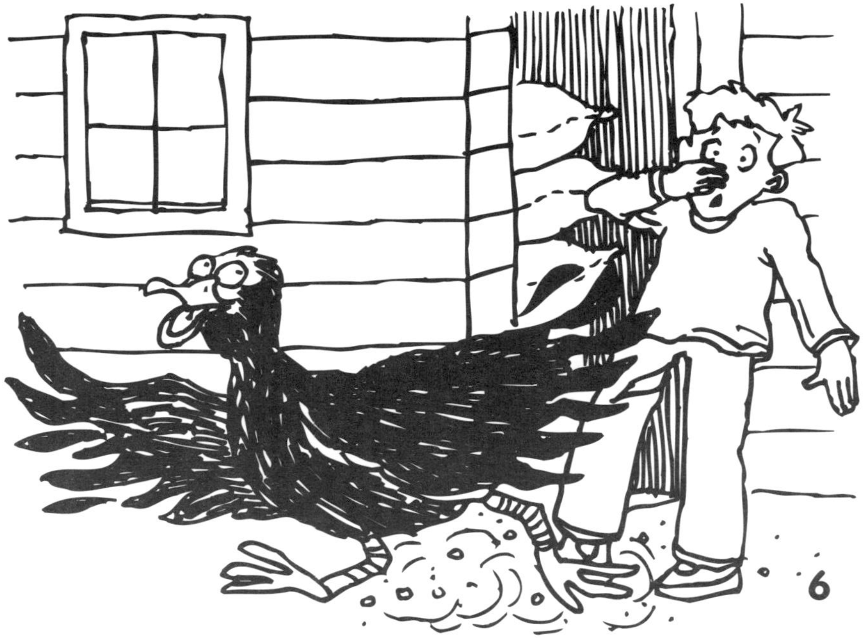

- Practice reading the **-ack** word family.
- Draw a line under words in the story that rhyme with **Jack**.
- How do you think the duck got into the sack?

Word Box

Jack	stack	quack
shack	sack	
back	black	

fold 2

2

"What is in that sack?" Jack asked himself.

As Jack looked in the sack, a big black duck bit him on his nose.

3

4

The duck hopped out of the sack and ran away.

5

-ain family

Jane's Trip

1

Jane is going to Spain.
She is going by train.

Jane is late for the train.
Oh no! It is starting to rain.

Think About It

- Practice reading the **-ain** word family.
- Draw a line under words in the story that rhyme with **rain**.
- Do you think Jane will get to Spain?

Word Box

brain	pain
rain	
sprain	
Jane	
Spain	
train	

6

2

3

Jane tripped in the rain.
Ow! What pain!
Jane has a sprain.
Jane missed the train.

fold 2

fold 2

fold 1

4

Use your brain.
Don't run in the rain!

5

Basic Phonics Skills, Level D • EMC 3321 • ©2004 by Evan-Moor Corp.

1

The blare of the truck's horn
scared the mare.

She jumped out of her square
pen and ran into the woods.

-are family

Rescue

— fold 2 —

— fold 2 —

fold 1

6

Think About It

- Practice reading the **-are** word family.
- Draw a line under words in the story that rhyme with **mare.**
- Why do you think the hunter set a snare in the woods?

Word Box

mare	square	flare
scare	stare	dare
blare	snare	care

2

3

Harry ran after the mare.
He stopped in his tracks
and stared.

The mare was caught in a
snare some hunter had set.

Harry set off a flare to get help.

"Do I dare try to help her?"
he asked himself.

4

Harry spoke to the mare.
"Don't be scared. I will take
care of you."

Soon, help arrived. They set
the mare free and took her
back to the farm.

5

Basic Phonics Skills, Level D • EMC 3321 • ©2004 by Evan-Moor Corp.

Making Repairs

"There are many things around this old house that I must repair," said Dad.

Some of the stair steps were broken. The cover on one chair was ripped.

A pair of posts on the front porch needed paint.

1

Think About It

- Practice reading the **-air** word family.
- Draw a line under words in the story that rhyme with **fair**.
- Do you think it was unfair of Dad to ask Max to help?

Word Box

repair	pair	unfair
stair	fair	despair
chair	air	

6

3

"We'll make repairs on Saturday," Dad told Max.

"That's not fair!" complained Max. "That's when I was going to meet my friends."

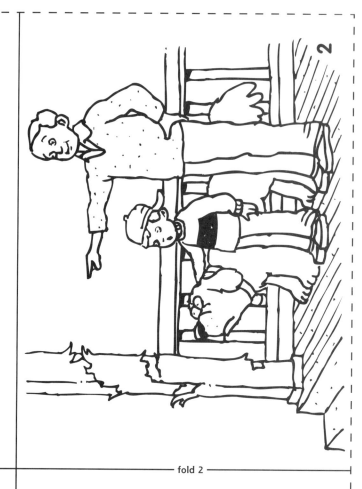

2

"I'm sorry, Max. But it's not unfair to ask you to help," said Dad.

"Don't despair. We'll repair things in the morning. Then you will be as free as the air after lunch."

5

4

Basic Phonics Skills, Level D • EMC 3321 • ©2004 by Evan-Moor Corp.

Dear Jim,

Did you hear?

This year we went camping.

Pen Pals

fold 2

fold 2

fold 1

Think About It

- Practice reading the **-ear** word family.
- Draw a line under words in the story that rhyme with **dear**.
- What would you write to a pen pal?

Word Box

hear	rear
near	year
gear	Dear

6

3

We threw our gear in the rear
of the truck.
And away we went.

2

4

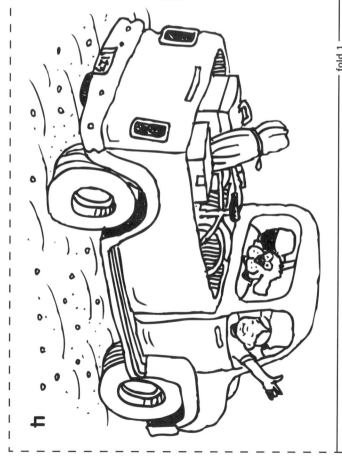

5

We camped near the lake.
It was fun.

Basic Phonics Skills, Level D • EMC 3321 • ©2004 by Evan-Moor Corp.

1

What did you do today?

What Did You Do Today?

-ead family

---

fold 2

fold 2

---

fold 1

Think About It

- Practice reading the **-ead** word family.
- Draw a line under words in the story that rhyme with **head**.
- What did you do today?

Word Box

spread   thread
bread   tread
read   head

I put my cap on my head
and went to the park.

That's what we did today.

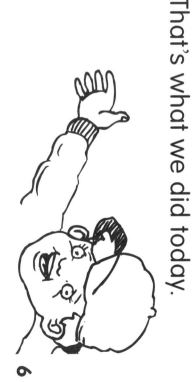

6

3

I read a book.

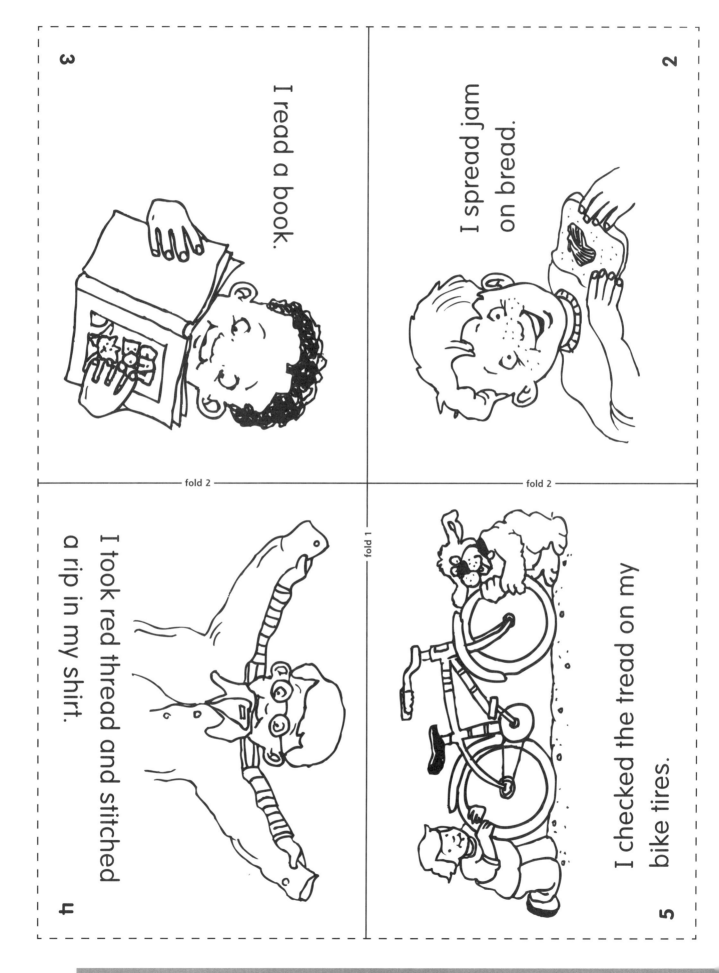

2

I spread jam
on bread.

fold 2

fold 2

fold 1

I took red thread and stitched
a rip in my shirt.

4

I checked the tread on my
bike tires.

5

1

The pirate crew was hungry. But few of them knew how to cook.

A Hungry Crew

-ew family

— fold 2 —

— fold 2 —

6

They picked up the poor cook and threw him overboard.

— fold 1 —

Think About It

- Practice reading the **-ew** word family.
- Draw a line under words in the story that rhyme with **crew**.
- What would you cook for the crew? Would they like it?

Word Box		
crew	new	blew
few	stew	chew
knew	brew	threw

3

The new cook made a hot stew. "I'll brew some tea, too," he said.

2

The captain pointed to a new crew member and shouted, "You! Cook for the crew."

fold 2 — fold 2

fold 1

4

The crew blew on their hot stew and started to chew.

5

"Yuck! This is terrible!" shouted the pirates.

Basic Phonics Skills, Level D • EMC 3321 • ©2004 by Evan-Moor Corp.

-eed family

Speedy

When he was young, Speedy could run faster than all of the other horses. That is how he got his name.

At races, people would shout, "Look at that speedy steed go!"

- Practice reading the -eed word family.
- Draw a line under words in the story that rhyme with **feed**.
- What else might Speedy need?

Think About It

Word Box

steed	speed	need
weed	freed	
reed	feed	

6

Little Phonics Readers 253

3

Now, Speedy was old. He wasn't fast anymore. No more races for Speedy. He just spent his days nibbling on a weed here and there.

One day, he got stuck in a pond. His feet were tangled in the reeds.

2

— fold 2 —

— fold 2 —

fold 1

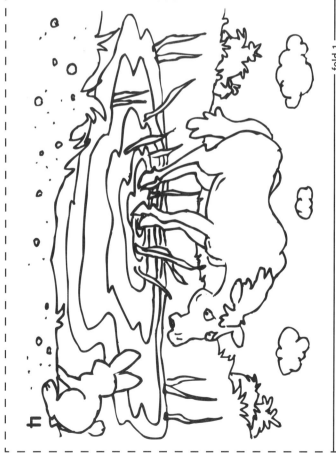

4

Along came the rancher. He freed Speedy from the reeds.

He took the tired old horse back to the barn to feed him oats and hay.

"That's just what I need," thought Speedy.

5

Little Phonics Readers   Basic Phonics Skills, Level D • EMC 3321 • ©2004 by Evan-Moor Corp.

-oy family

A Toy for Roy

1

"We have a new baby boy,"
said Mother. "He fills our
hearts with joy!"

They named the new boy
Roy after his grandfather.

---

fold 2 ——— | ——— fold 2

fold 1

Think About It

- Practice reading the **-oy** word family.
- Draw a line under words in the story that rhyme with **toy**.
- What kind of toy would you give to a baby?

Word Box	
boy	Troy
joy	toy
Roy	enjoy

6

6

3

Troy came to visit the baby boy.
"Here is a toy for little Roy," he said.

2

4

5

"I think he will enjoy it," said Troy.
Roy smiled and grabbed for the toy.

Basic Phonics Skills, Level D • EMC 3321 • ©2004 by Evan-Moor Corp.

1

Rub oil on the meat and put it in a pan.

Put the pan under the hot coil in the oven to broil the meat.

Don't broil it too long or it will spoil the meat.

-oil family

Boil and Broil

— fold 2 —

— fold 2 —

fold 1

- Practice reading the **-oil** word family.
- Draw a line under words in the story that rhyme with **oil**.
- What would you cook for dinner?

Think About It

Word Box

oil	spoil	
broil	boil	
coil	foil	

6

Boil rice while the meat cooks.

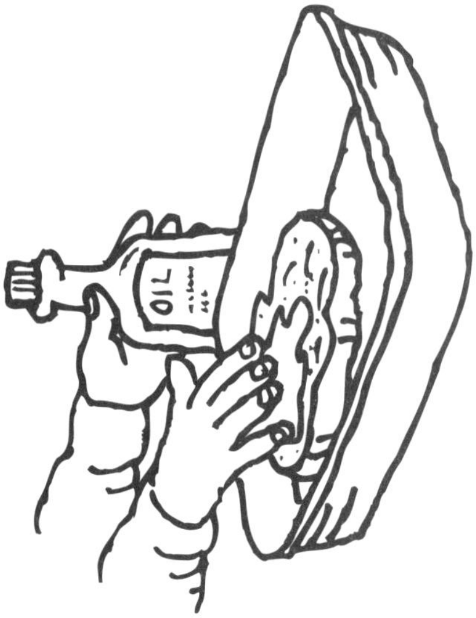

fold 2

fold 2

fold 1

4

Put the broiled meat and boiled rice on the table.

Enjoy your meal!

Wrap any leftover meat in foil. Store it in the freezer.

5

Basic Phonics Skills, Level D • EMC 3321 • ©2004 by Evan-Moor Corp.

Stuck in the Sludge

-udge family

One cold winter day, Judge Jones was driving home from work.

Suddenly, he hit ice on the road.

His car skidded off the road.

The car got stuck in the muddy sludge on the side of the road.

1

6

Think About It

- Practice reading the **-udge** word family.
- Draw a line under words in the story that rhyme with **fudge.**
- How do you think the driver got the judge's car out of the sludge?

Word Box

judge   budge
sludge   trudge
fudge

2

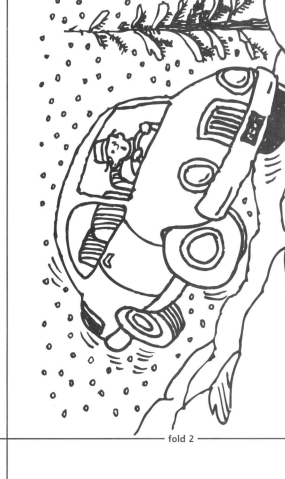

— fold 2 —

— fold 1 —

3

"Oh, fudge!" shouted the judge. He tried to start the car. It wouldn't budge.

The judge got out of the car. He began to trudge to town for help.

4

5

A jeep stopped and picked him up. "I'll help you," said the driver.

Soon, the judge's car was out of the sludge. The judge was on his way home again.

A Fright in the Night

-**ight** family

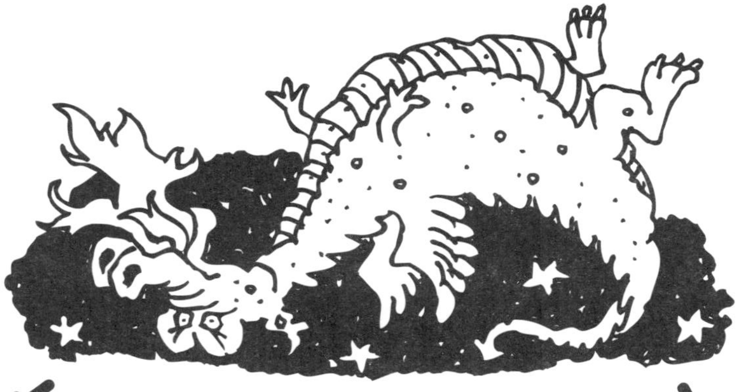

A knight was going back to the castle. It was late on a very dark night.

Suddenly, he saw a bright light far off.

"What was that?" he said. "I must get closer so I can see."

1

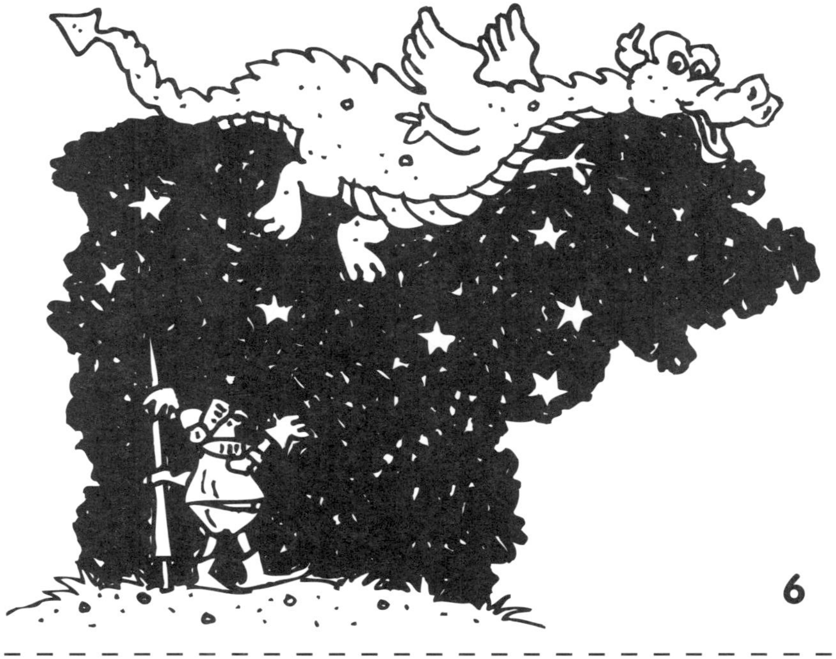

6

Think About It

- Practice reading the **-ight** word family.
- Draw a line under words in the story that rhyme with **light**.
- Why do you think the dragon took flight?

Word Box

fright	bright	light
night	fight	tonight
knight	flight	

fold 1

fold 2

3

The knight got a bad fright.
The light had come from
a dragon.

"What am I going to do?"
said the knight. "I don't want
to fight a dragon tonight."

2

fold 2

fold 2

fold 1

4

Just then, the dragon took
flight. The knight did not have
to fight that night.

5

   Basic Phonics Skills, Level D • EMC 3321 • ©2004 by Evan-Moor Corp.

In My Soup

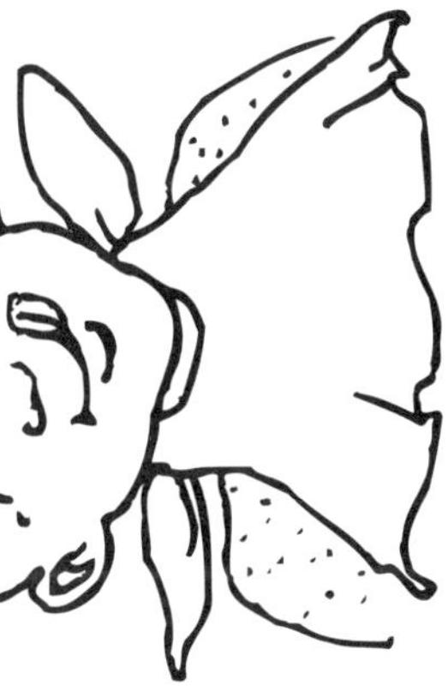

Coop had alphabet soup
for lunch.

"Wow!" said Coop with a
whoop. "I see my name in
this soup." He ate his name.

1

6

- Practice reading the **-oop**
  word family.
- Draw a line under words in the
  story that rhyme with **hoop**.
- What words do you think Coop
  will find in his new bowl of soup?

Think About It

Word Box

coop   troop
scoop   whoop

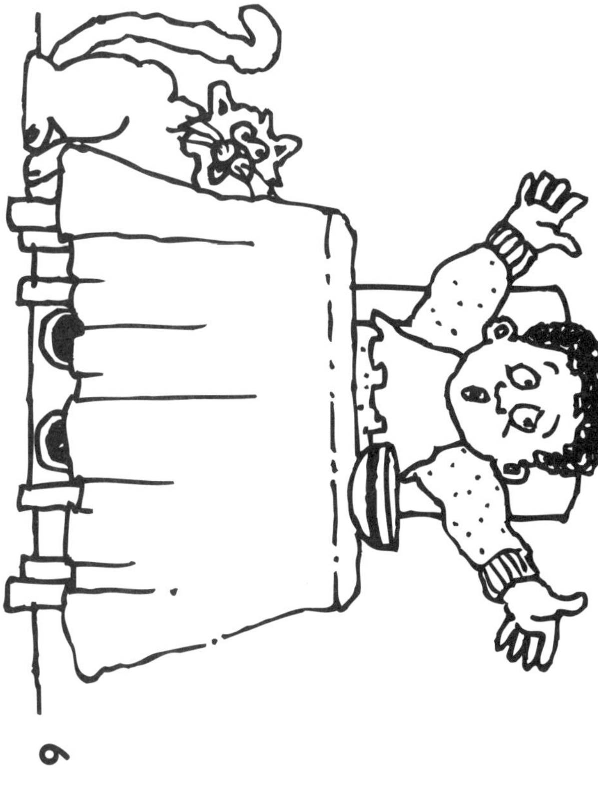

3

"Now I see **scoop**." Coop
scooped up **s-c-o-o-p**
and ate it.

"Here is **troop**." Coop ate it
letter by letter.

2

4

"My soup is all gone," said Coop.

"Mom, may I please have more
soup?" he asked.

5

Brooke Cooks

Brooke likes to cook.

I think I'll
make raisin
bread today.

1

She let the
baked bread
cool. Then
she took a
big slice and
ate it. Yum!

6

- Practice reading the **-ook**
  word family.
- Draw a line under words in the
  story that rhyme with **cook**.
- What do you like to cook?

Think About It

Word Box

	took	nook
	look	shook
Brooke	hook	
cook		
cookbook		

3

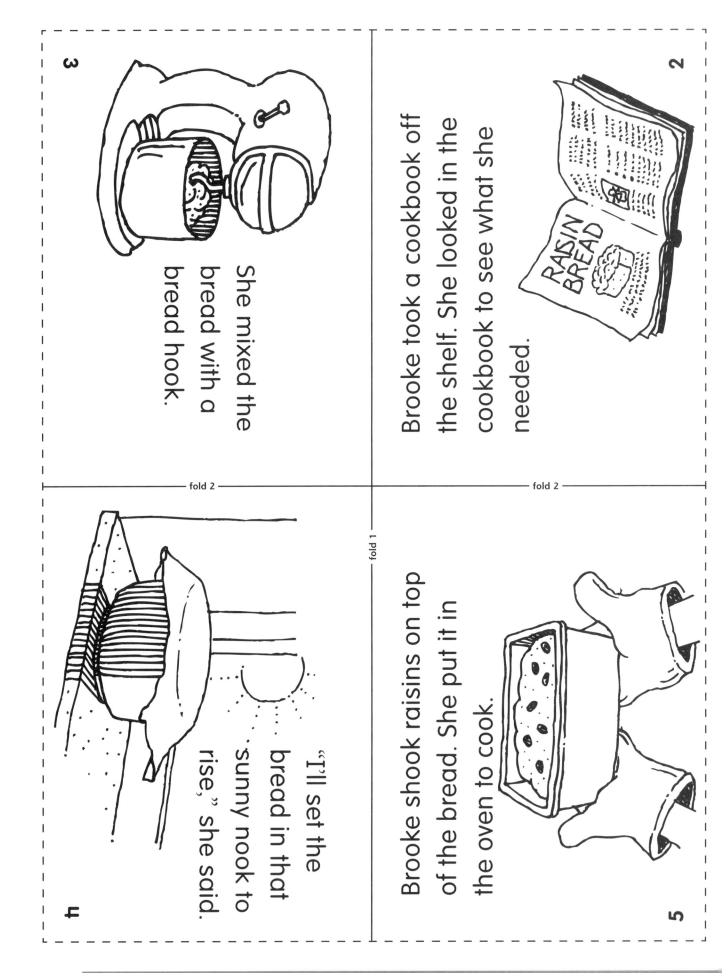

She mixed the bread with a bread hook.

2

Brooke took a cookbook off the shelf. She looked in the cookbook to see what she needed.

fold 2

fold 2

fold 1

4

"I'll set the bread in that sunny nook to rise," she said.

5

Brooke shook raisins on top of the bread. She put it in the oven to cook.

Basic Phonics Skills, Level D • EMC 3321 • ©2004 by Evan-Moor Corp.

Do you know how flowers grow?

Sow the seeds row by row.

Mary's Garden

fold 2

fold 2

fold 1

Think About It

- Practice reading the **-ow** word family.
- Draw a line under words in the story that rhyme with **grow.**
- What kind of flowers would you like to grow?

Word Box		
grow	slow	know
sow	show	yellow
row	bow	

6

2

3

Water them and watch them grow. I can't wait. It seems so slow.

At last, the flowers start to show!

4

Pick a bunch. Tie them with a yellow bow.

Give them to someone special you know.

5

   Basic Phonics Skills, Level D • EMC 3321 • ©2004 by Evan-Moor Corp.

Farmer Brown

Farmer Brown is a busy man.
There is a lot of work to do
on a farm.

1

• Practice reading the **-ow** word family.

• Draw a line under words in the story that rhyme with **cow**.

• What other animals might be on Farmer Brown's farm?

Think About It

Word Box

cow	brow	
sow	chow	
plow	now	

How about some chow?

Now?

9

3

Next, he feeds the sow and her piglets.

2

Every day he must milk the cow.

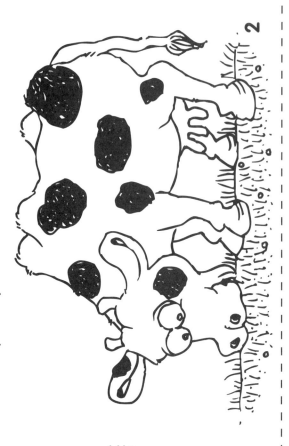

— fold 2 —

— fold 2 —

— fold 1 —

4

Then he must plow the field.

5

Farmer Brown wipes his brow.

WHEW! I'M TIRED.

Trout Fishing

1

A Boy Scout went to the river to fish.

He threw his line into the water. Soon, he started to shout, "I caught a trout!"

The Scout pulled the trout out of the water.

6

Think About It

- Practice reading the **-ow** word family.

- Draw a line under words in the story that rhyme with **Scout**.

- Do you think the Boy Scout will sell the trout to the stout man?

Word Box

Scout	out
trout	stout
shout	about

2

3

A stout man was fishing in the river, too. He had not caught a fish.

"That's a nice trout," said the stout man. "How about selling it to me?"

4

"I'll think about it," said the boy as he threw his line back into the water.

5

1

Pete had an old hound dog.
The hound ran across the ground. Then he ran up a mound of dirt.

-ound family

Pete's Hound Dog

fold 2

---

fold 2

fold 1

- Practice reading the **-ound** word family.
- Draw a line under words in the story that rhyme with **round**.
- Why do you think Pete called his hound silly?

Think About It

Word Box

hound	around	wound
mound	sound	unwound
ground	found	

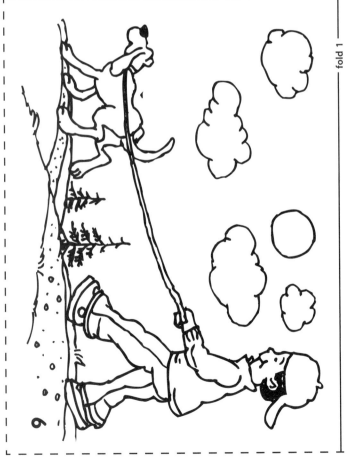

6

3

His leash got stuck on a pole. Around and around he ran.

He wound his leash around the pole. "Owooo!" What a sound he made.

2

4

5

Pete found his hound. He unwound the leash.

"Let's go home, you silly hound," said Pete. And off they went.

fold 2

fold 2

fold 1

-ark family

One Bark in the Dark

1

Clark's dog Spark was lost. It was dark now, and Clark still could not find his pet.

"Where can Spark be?" Clark asked his dad. "Will we ever find him?"

6

Think About It

- Practice reading the -ark word family.
- Draw a line under words in the story that rhyme with **dark**.
- How do you think Spark got lost?

Word Box

bark	Spark
dark	park
Clark	mark

Late that night, after he went to bed, Clark heard a dog bark. The sound came from deep in the park next to Clark's house.

Clark and his dad went into the dark park. They saw the mark of dog paws in the dirt. Clark kept calling Spark's name.

3

2

Soon, a barking dog was jumping up on Clark. "Where have you been, you silly dog?" said Clark as he hugged his pet.

5

Basic Phonics Skills, Level D • EMC 3321 • ©2004 by Evan-Moor Corp.

What's the Score?

-ore family

More than
anything,
Jim wanted
to score a
run for his
team.

1

---

fold 2

fold 2

fold 1

• Practice reading the **-ore** word family.

• Draw a line under words in the story that rhyme with **more**.

• How did Jim hurt himself?

Think About It

Word Box

score	tore
more	wore
before	sore

Will I be able to score a run with a sore leg?

Yes, he was able to score a run for his team.

6

3

He tore his shirt. The cap he wore fell into the dirt.

2

Jim ran to the ballpark. Before he got to the park, Jim fell down.

fold 2

fold 2

fold 1

4

When he stood up, his leg was sore.

5

Will I be able to play with a sore leg?

Yes, he was able to play with his team.

Basic Phonics Skills, Level D • EMC 3321 • ©2004 by Evan-Moor Corp.

Answer Key

Page 8: 1. /k/; 2. /s/; 3. /k/; 4. /k/; 5. /k/; 6. /s/; 7. /s/; 8. /k/; 9. /k/

Page 9: **/k/:** castle, catnip, because, candle, uncle, pecan, curb; **/s/:** race, cereal, princess, fancy, icy, decide, pencil, celery

Page 10: 1. cabin; 2. cucumber; 3. rice; 4. cider; 5. pack; 6. cupcakes; 7. buckle; 8. slice

Page 11: Answers will vary, but should contain the given words.

Page 12: 1. /j/; 2. /g/; 3. /j/; 4. /g/; 5. /j/; 6. /g/; 7. /g/; 8. /j/; 9. /g/

Page 13: **/j/:** giraffe, sponge, gem, page, ginger, huge, gym; **/g/:** tiger, gum, frog, wagon, flag, sugar, gave

Page 14: 1. danger; 2. giggles; 3. rag; 4. nugget; 5. soggy; 6. ledge; 7. ranger; 8. hinge; 9. iguana; 10. garage

Page 15: Answers will vary, but should contain the given words.

Page 16: 1. /zh/; 2. /s/; 3. /s/; 4. /z/; 5. /z/; 6. /s/; 7. /s/; 8. /z/; 9. /sh/

Page 17: **/s/:** sink, miss, glass; **/sh/:** sugar, sure, tissue; **/s/:** wise, easy, raisin; **/zh/:** measure, treasure, pleasure

Page 18: 1. raisin; 2. tissue; 3. fossil; 4. treasure; 5. please; 6. nurse; 7. wise; 8. invisible

Page 19: 1. music; 2. case; 3. keys; 4. roses; 5. surprised; 6. museum; 7. pleasure; 8. famous

Page 20: mouse, cheese, sugar, treasure— Answers will vary, but must contain all the given words.

Page 21: 1. cent; 2. wag; 3. ice; 4. gem; 5. gum; 6. nose; 7. gas; 8. mice; 9. page; 10. cheese; 11. race; 12. cup; 13. cage; 14. game

Page 22: 1. frog; 2. corn; 3. pencil; 4. giraffe; 5. rose; 6. wagon; 7. giant; 8. city; 9. hose; 10. tissue

Page 23: 1. /ch/; 2. /sh/; 3. /k/; 4. /k/; 5. /k/; 6. /ch/; 7. /ch/; 8. /ch/; 9. /ch/

Page 24: **/ch/:** church, ranch, peach, change, cheetah, chest, chowder, chapter; **/sh/:** chiffon, chute; **/k/:** chemical, stomach

Page 25: 1. I am a peach; 2. I am a parachute; 3. I am a cheetah; 4. I am a chimney; 5. I am an anchor; 6. I am a branch; 7. I am a chef; 8. I am a machine.

Page 26: Answers will vary, but should contain the given words.

Page 27: 1. unvoiced; 2. unvoiced; 3. unvoiced; 4. voiced; 5. unvoiced; 6. unvoiced; 7. unvoiced; 8. voiced; 9. voiced

Page 28: 1. yes; 2. yes; 3. no; 4. yes; 5. yes; 6. no; 7. yes; 8. no; 9. no; 10. no

Page 29: 1. tooth; 2. thunder; 3. theater; 4. brother; 5. math; 6. bath; 7. wreath; 8. third; 9. Thank; 10. weather

Page 30: thief, thirteen, toothbrush, brothers— Answers will vary, but must contain all the given words.

Page 31: 1. third; 2. cherry; 3. chair, bench; 4. thin; 5. March; 6. thief; 7. chef; 8. chicken; 9. children; 10. math

Page 32: 1. feathers; 2. choir; 3. father; 4. chop; 5. stomach; 6. beach; 7. bath; 8. thousand; 9. thunder; 10. think

Page 33:

Page 34: 1. decoration—yes; 2. lotion—yes; 3. ticket—no; 4. delicious—yes; 5. musician—yes; 6. signal—no; 7. nation—yes; 8. mission—yes; 9. cinnamon roll—no

Page 35: 1. lotion; 2. nation; 3. social; 4. action; 5. potion; 6. fraction; 7. subtraction; 8. addition; 9. station; 10. special; A car-nation

Page 36: 1. transportation; 2. directions; 3. glacier; 4. delicious; 5. illustration; 6. lotion; 7. nation; 8. fraction

Page 37: Answers will vary, but should contain the given words.

Page 39: 1. lam**b**; 2. clim**b**; 3. com**b**; 4. lim**b**; 5. thum**b**; 6. club (crossed out); 1. lamb; 2. comb; 3. climb

Page 40: Words should be matched with their pictures—1. crumb; 2. lamb; 3. thumb; 4. limb; 5. comb; 6. climb; climb, limb

Page 41: 1. comb; 2. lamb; 3. crumb; 4. thumb; 5. limb; 6. climb; **Silent letters:** clim**b**, thum**b**, lim**b**, plum**b**er; **Circled:** bulb, lamp, branch, rubber

Page 42: 1. **h**onest; 2. **rh**ino; 3. cheeta**h**; 4. **h**our; 5. g**h**ost; 6. hand (crossed out); 1. hour; 2. cheetah; 3. ghost

Page 43: Words should be matched with their pictures—1. rhino; 2. cheetah; 3. hour; 4. rhubarb; 5. ghost; 6. honest; rhubarb, hour

Page 44: 1. hour; 2. cheetah; 3. honest; 4. ghost; 5. rhyme; 6. rhubarb; 7. rhinoceros; 8. herb

Page 45: 1. autum**n**; 2. seven (crossed out); 3. colum**n**; 4. pencil (crossed out); 5. hym**n**; 6. man (crossed out); 1. autumn; 2. hymn; 3. column

Page 46: 1. autumn; 2. comb; 3. honest; 4. thumb; 5. rhyme; 6. lamb; 7. climb; 8. limb

Page 47: 1. **g**naw; 2. **g**nome; 3. gift (crossed out); 4. si**g**n; 5. **g**nat; 6. **g**nu; 1. gnaw; 2. sign; 3. gnu

Page 48: 1. **k**nife; 2. king (crossed out); 3. **k**nob; 4. **k**night; 5. **k**nee; 6. **k**not; 1. knot; 2. knob; 3. knife

Page 49: Words should be matched with their pictures—1. **k**nife; 2. **g**nome; 3. **k**nit; 4. **g**nat; 5. **k**nock; 6. **k**not; 7. **k**nee; 8. **k**nob

Page 50: 1. knit; 2. gnu; 3. knife; 4. knights; 5. gnaws; 6. gnats

Page 51: **g**nome, **k**nuckles, **g**nawed, **g**narly, **g**nats, **G**nashing, **k**nock, **k**neel, **g**nome

Page 52: 1. **sc**ent; 2. **sc**ientist; 3. camp (crossed out); 4. **sc**issors; 5. mus**c**les; 6. **sc**epter; 1. muscles; 2. scissors; 3. scepter

Page 53: 1. scenery; 2. scent; 3. science; 4. scissors; 5. muscles; 6. scepter

Page 54: Words should be matched to their pictures—1. scissors; 2. muscles; 3. scepter; 4. scent; 5. scenery; muscles

Page 55: 1. **w**ren; 2. wagon (crossed out); 3. **w**rench; 4. **w**rist; 5. **w**reath; 6. **w**rote; 1. wrench; 2. wrote; 3. wreath

Page 56: Words should be matched with their pictures—1. wrist; 2. write; 3. wreck; 4. wreath; 5. wren; 6. wrench; wren, wreath

Page 57: 1. wrapper; 2. wrinkles; 3. wrong; 4. wrote; 5. wreck; 6. wrist; 7. wrap; 8. write; 9. writing

Page 58: 1. wrench; 2. wren; 3. wrapped; 4. wrote; 5. wrinkles; 6. who; 7. wriggled; 8. wrong; 9. whole; 10. wreath

Page 59: 1. fu**dg**e; 2. bri**dg**e; 3. ju**dg**e; 4. glad (crossed out); 5. ba**dg**e; 6. he**dg**e; 1. fudge; 2. hedge; 3. bridge

Basic Phonics Skills, Level D • EMC 3321 • ©2004 by Evan-Moor Corp.

Page 60: Words should be matched with their pictures—1. fudge; 2. badge; 3. judge; 4. bridge; 5. hedge; 6. wedge; badge, bridge

Page 61: 1. judge; 2. fudge; 3. badge; 4. hedge; 5. bridge; 6. nudge; 7. badger; 8. wedge

Page 62: 1. half; 2. yolk; 3. wall (crossed out); 4. calf; 5. salmon; 6. chalk; 1. calf; 2. chalk; 3. talk

Page 63: Words should be matched with their pictures—1. chalk; 2. walk; 3. talk; 4. calf; 5. half; 6. salmon; salmon, half

Page 64: 1. yolk; 2. chalk; 3. talk; 4. salmon; 5. calf; 6. half; 7. stalks; 8. walk

Page 65: 1. whistle; 2. watch; 3. castle; 4. heart (crossed out); 5. wrestle; 6. listen; 1. whistle; 2. listen; 3. castle

Page 66: Words should be matched with their pictures—1. wrestle; 2. watch; 3. castle; 4. listen; 5. fasten; 6. whistle; listen, watch

Page 67: 1. soften; 2. fasten; 3. whistle; 4. hatchet; 5. batch; 6. castle; 7. catch; 8. listen

Page 68: 1. flight; 2. night; 3. eight; 4. straight; 5. light; 6. ghost (crossed out); 1. straight; 2. eight; 3. night

Page 69: Words should be matched with their pictures—1. eight; 2. night; 3. high; 4. flight; 5. straight; 6. light; light

Page 70: 1. high; 2. straight; 3. light; 4. tight; 5. right; 6. night

Page 71: 1. weighs; 2. listen; 3. calf; 4. fight; 5. straight; 6. walk; 7. often; 8. would; 9. patches

Page 72: 1. fasten; 2. latch; 3. half; 4. talked; 5. salmon; 6. high; 7. fright; 8. walked

Page 73: **Silent b:** lamb, comb, thumb; **Silent h:** rhino, ghost, cheetah; **Silent n:** hymn, column, autumn; **Silent k:** knife, knee, knot

Page 74: **Silent g:** sign, gnome, gnaw, gnat; **Silent d:** fudge, judge; **Silent c:** muscle, scissors, scent; **Silent w:** wrote, wrist, wrench

Page 75: **Silent t:** listen, castle, wrestle; **Silent l:** yolk, talk, calf; **Silent b:** comb, lamb, climb; **Silent gh:** light, flight, high

Page 76: 1. comb; 2. hour; 3. rhino; 4. autumn; 5. thumb; 6. crumb; 7. column; 8. cheetah; 9. ghost; 10. candy (crossed out); 11. honest; 12. paper (crossed out)

Page 77: 1. knob; 2. gnaw; 3. bread (crossed out); 4. knock; 5. knot; 6. sign; 7. knife; 8. knee; 9. bug (crossed out); 10. scissors; 11. muscles; 12. craft (crossed out)

Page 78: 1. wren; 2. plant (crossed out); 3. fudge; 4. write; 5. half; 6. happy (crossed out); 7. wrist; 8. bridge; 9. yolk; 10. wrench; 11. judge; 12. calf

Page 79: 1. whistle; 2. watch; 3. wagon (crossed out); 4. night; 5. ghost; 6. listen; 7. eight; 8. high; 9. right; 10. run (crossed out); 11. knee; 12. knot

Page 80: Answers will vary, but should contain the given words.

Page 82: 1. tail; 2. drain; 3. bait; 4. sail; 5. hail; 6. gray; 7. nail; 8. tray

Page 83: 1. paid; 2. grain; 3. trail; 4. wail; 5. nail; 6. gray; 7. drain; 8. mail

Page 84:

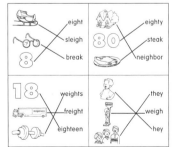

Page 85: **eigh**t **eigh**ty br**ea**k n**eigh** pr**ey** sl**eigh** gr**ea**t n**eigh**bor **eigh**teen wh**ey**
1. **eigh**t, **eigh**ty, **eigh**teen; 2. br**ea**k; 3. n**eigh**bor; 4. sl**eigh**; 5. pr**ey**; 6. n**eigh**; 7. wh**ey**; 8. gr**ea**t

Page 86: 1. great; 2. eight; 3. neighborhood; 4. sleigh; 5. break; 6. steak; 7. weights; 8. eighty

Page 87: Answers will vary, but should contain the given words.

Page 88:

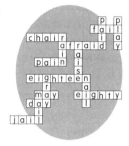

Page 89: 1. great; 2. bait; 3. hail; 4. tail; 5. pray; 6. grain; 7. main; 8. away; 9. paint; long a

Page 90:

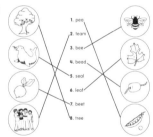

Page 91: p**ea**k b**ea**ver cl**ea**n b**ee**p gr**ee**n f**ea**st g**ee**se w**ee**p **ea**gle kn**ea**d
1. clean; 2. weep; 3. feast; 4. eagle; 5. green; 6. beep; 7. beaver; 8. knead; 9. geese; 10. peak

Page 92: 1. teeth; 2. tear; 3. clear; 4. dream; 5. peel; 6. beef; 7. weed; 8. creak; 9. steep; 10. sea

Page 93: 1. collie, monkey, donkey; 2. chief; 3. key; 4. field; 5. niece; 6. thief; 7. piece; 8. money

Page 94: 1. key; 2. shield; 3. monkey; 4. honey; 5. chief; 6. piece; 7. field; 8. money; 9. donkey

Page 95: 1. piece; 2. key; 3. field; 4. collie; 5. niece; 6. donkey; 7. believe; 8. chimney; 9. money

Page 96: Answers will vary, but should contain the given words.

Page 97:

H	A	N	D	K	E	R	C	H	I	E	F	R	X
O	J	I	R	Z	L	B	O	D	X	L	E	A	P
N	C	R	E	A	K	G	O	R	H	E	A	M	D
E	Q	E	A	C	O	M	K	C	B	F	S	P	W
Y	F	K	M	B	Y	S	I	T	E	E	T	H	E
A	S	I	M	O	N	K	E	Y	L	J	J	H	A
T	M	R	I	Q	R	G	K	T	I	F	Q	Y	S
L	E	A	V	E	S	N	G	E	E	S	E	P	E
Z	A	S	L	D	H	S	R	V	V	G	H	A	L
T	L	T	N	P	I	V	E	M	E	A	T	K	M
E	V	E	X	B	E	O	E	W	Z	U	L	J	W
N	W	E	V	D	L	C	N	Y	A	F	B	X	O
U	S	P	E	E	D	M	C	G	W	E	A	V	E

Page 98: 1. key; 2. bee; 3. money; 4. jeep; 5. feet; 6. leaf; 7. deer; 8. pea; 9. donkey; 10. teeth; 11. cookie; 12. monkey

Page 99: 1. pie; 2. eye; 3. tie; 4. good-bye; 5. guy; 6. rye; 7. buy; 8. lie; 9. flies

Page 100: 1. die, pie, lie, tie, fried; 2. guy, buy; 3. rye, dye, good-bye; 4. pie; 5. guy; 6. good-bye; 7. rye; 8. buy

Page 101: 1. die; 2. eyes; 3. pie; 4. dyed; 5. guy; 6. lie; 7. rye; 8. buy; 9. tie; 10. good-bye

Page 102: Answers will vary, but should contain the given words.

Page 103:

buy	eye	cried	ridge	trick	spin
tin	big	lye	guy	fried	rye
dip	field	bridge	bring	lit	fried
trip	gift	sing	tie	dye	flies
shin	twist	wish	die	pit	will
cliff	zipper	hill	lie	pie	FINISH

Page 104: 1. toe; 2. road; 3. row; 4. bowl; 5. toad; 6. hoe; toad, row

Page 105:

Page 106: 1. window; 2. oatmeal; 3. toe; 4. grow; 5. blow; 6. bow; 7. soap; 8. road

Page 107: Answers will vary, but should contain the given words.

Page 108: 1. mow; 2. roast; 3. grown; 4. blow; 5. boat; 6. bowl; 7. soap; 8. hoe; 9. doe

Page 109: 1. sn**ow**, c**oa**t; 2. gr**ow**n, **Joe**; 3. t**oe**s; 4. m**ow**, s**oa**ked; 5. b**owl**, C**oa**ch, t**oa**st; 6. t**ow**, R**oa**d; 7. l**oa**n; 8. l**oa**f, gr**ow**n; 9. J**oa**n, gr**oa**ned, g**oa**l; 10. d**oe**, kn**ow**s

Page 110: 1. d; 2. g; 3. h; 4. c; 5. b; 6. f; 7. a; 8. i; 9. j; 10. e

Page 111:

Page 112: 1. newspaper; 2. clues; 3. overdue; 4. glue; 5. flew; 6. knew; 7. threw; 8. drew

Page 113: Answers will vary, but should contain at least 5 words from the word box.

Page 114: Answers will vary, but should correctly spell -*ue* and -*ew* words.

Page 115: Words should be matched with their pictures—head, feather, bread, spread, thread; 1. feather, head; 2. Spread, bread; 3. thread

Page 116: 1. guinea pig; 2. quilt; 3. thread; 4. ahead; 5. bread; 6. cousin; 7. tough; 8. leather; 9. touch

Page 117: 1. head; 2. touch; 3. built; 4. quilt; 5. feather; 6. ready; 7. rough; 8. thread; 9. count

Page 118:

Page 119: 1. j**aw**; 2. s**aw**; 3. c**au**ght; 4. h**aw**k; 5. s**au**sage; 6. p**aw**; 7. str**aw**; 8. f**au**cet; 9. cl**aw**

Page 120: 1. hawk; 2. auto; 3. daughter; 4. crawl; 5. dawn; 6. claw; 7. paw; 8. draw; 9. straw; 10. saw

Page 121: 1. crawl; 2. straw; 3. claws; 4. paw; 5. saw; 6. haul; 7. caught; 8. jaws

Page 122: Answers will vary, but should contain the given words.

Page 123: 1. moon; 2. broom; 4. tooth; 6. pool; 8. spool; 9. boot

Page 124: Circled (20 words total): Hood, woods, brook, hook, nook, cookbook, cookies, Woof, footsteps, good

Page 125: **Spoon:** boot, noon, tool, zoo, tooth, troop, goose; **Hook:** book, wood, foot, brook, cook

Page 126: **Underlined:** 1. hook; 5. foot; 7. wood; 11. book; 15. cook; **Circled:** 2. boot; 3. goose; 4. roof; 6. hoop; 8. moon; 9. spool; 10. tooth; 12. spoon; 13. tools; 14. broom; 16. moose

Page 127: 1. di**sh**; 2. **ch**air; 3. **ch**ain; 4. **ch**ild; 5. **sh**ip; 6. **ch**est; 7. **sh**ell; 8. **ch**eese; 9. **sh**eep; 10. bran**ch**; 11. **sh**irt; 12. **sh**elves

Page 128: 1. **th**orn; 2. **th**irty; 3. **wh**eat; 4. **wh**ip; 5. **wh**eel; 6. too**th**; 7. **th**umb; 8. brea**th**; 9. **wh**iskers; 10. **th**imble; 11. **wh**ite; 12. nor**th**

Page 129: 1. sh; 2. sh; 3. ch; 4. th; 5. wh; 6. sh; 7. wh; 8. wh; 9. ch; 1. beach; 2. lunch; 3. sandwich; 4. bench

Page 130: 1. thick, whistle; 2. ship, when; 3. shell, cheer; 4. She, chain; 5. show, them

Page 131: 1. **ph**oto, beginning; 2. go**ph**er, middle; 3. **ph**one, beginning; 4. lau**gh**, end; 5. gra**ph**, end; 6. **ph**easant, beginning; 7. tro**ph**y, middle; 8. cou**gh**, end

Page 132: 1. **ph**one; 2. **ph**oto; 3. cou**gh**; 4. tou**gh**; 5. enou**gh**; 6. rou**gh**; 7. **ph**easant; 8. **ph**ony

Page 133: Sentences underlined: 1. The road is rough—rough; 2. That joke made Phil laugh—Phil, laugh; 3. She likes photos—photos; 4. She has a bad cough—cough

Page 135: 1. **oi**l, beginning; 2. b**oy**, end; 3. s**oi**l, middle; 4. c**oi**l, middle; 5. t**oy**, end; 6. c**oi**ns, middle; 7. b**oi**l, middle; 8. p**oi**nt, middle

Page 136: 1. poison; 2. coins; 3. joyful; 4. oyster; 5. toys; 6. point; 7. voyage; 8. choice; 9. destroy; 10. boy; 11. soil; 12. boil

Page 137: 1. oil; 2. join; 3. pointed; 4. destroyed; 5. coin; 6. voices; 7. choice; 8. joyful

Page 138: Answers will vary, but should contain the given words.

Page 139: 1. c; 2. g; 3. j; 4. d; 5. f; 6. a; 7. i; 8. e; 9. h; 10. b

Page 140: New words may vary, but should be spelled correctly—1. cow, how; 2. house, mouse; 3. couch, grouch; 4. mouth, south; 5. gown; town; 6. sour, hour; 7. cloud, loud; 8. bounce, pounce; 9. flour, scour; 10. scout, pout

Page 141: Answers will vary, but should contain at least 7 words from the word box.

Page 142: 1. house; 2. couch; 3. flour; 4. plow; 5. town; 6. pounced; 7. ground; 8. how; 9. bound; 10. frown

Page 143: Circled: 1. oil, brown; 2. boy; 3. coil, town; 4. mouth; 5. gown; point; 6. joy, count; 7. mouse, moist; 8. coin; 9. ground, growl

Page 144: 1. mouse; 2. clown; 3. coins; 4. gown; 5. boy; 6. trout; 7. soil; 8. cloud; 9. cow; 10. toy; 11. house; 12. mouth

Page 146: 1. farm; 2. harm; 3. charm; 4. start; 5. dart; 6. smart; 7. part; 8. lard; 9. hard; 10. card

Page 147: 1. market; 2. artist; 3. March; 4. cart; 5. carpet; 6. bark; 7. arm; 8. barn; 9. star; 10. marble

Page 148:

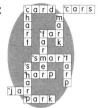

Page 149: Answers will vary, but should contain the given words.

Page 150: 1. fair; 2. hair; 3. pair; 4. stairs; 5. hare; 6. bear; 7. pear; 8. scare; 9. share

Page 151: 1. stairs; 2. rare; 3. pair; 4. scare; 5. dare; 6. stare; 7. lair; 8. Beware

Page 152: 1. ch**arm**; 2. m**are**; 3. h**ard**; 4. st**art**; 5. w**ear**; 6. p**ear**; 7. sh**are**; 8. d**art**

Page 153: 1. bark; 2. scare; 3. spare; 4. harm; 5. stars; 6. hare; 7. flare; 8. care; 9. cards; 10. pair

Page 154: 1. herb; 2. verb; 3. term; 4. germ; 5. jerk; 6. clerk; 7. fern; 8. herd; 9. her; 10. stern

Page 155: 1. p**er**fect; 2. sh**er**bet; 3. g**er**bil; 4. m**er**maid; 5. remem**b**er; 6. check**er**s; 7. n**er**vous; 8. s**er**vant; 9. lawy**er**; 10. h**er**d

Page 156: 1. bird; 2. third; 3. fir; 4. stir; 5. sir; 6. girl; 7. twirl; 8. firm

Page 157: **-irt:** dirt, shirt, skirt, squirt; **-irst:** first, thirst; 1. thirst; 2. dirt; 3. shirt; 4. first; 5. skirt; 6. squirt

Page 158: 1. fur; 2. purr; 3. burn; 4. hurry; 5. nurse; 6. turnip; 7. furniture; 8. turtle

Page 159:
Nurse Nancy needed a new <u>purse</u>. She went to the store. "It won't <u>hurt</u> to look here," she thought. So she combed her <u>curls</u> and walked in.

"What do you want?" asked a clerk.

"I want a new <u>purse</u>," said the <u>nurse</u>.

"Well, I have just the <u>purse</u> for you," the clerk <u>blurted</u> out. And she threw an old <u>purse</u> at <u>Nurse</u> Nancy. "It is a <u>purse</u> with a <u>curse</u>!"

<u>Nurse</u> Nancy was not afraid. "This <u>purse</u> cannot <u>hurt</u> me," she said. So she reached inside. She felt something squishy. <u>Nurse</u> Nancy screamed and <u>hurled</u> the purse far away.

What was in the <u>purse</u>, you ask?

It was just <u>yogurt</u>!

1. nurse; 2. yogurt; 3. purse; 4. curse;
5. hurt; 6. blurted

Page 160: 1. birthday; 2. flurries; 3. twirled;
4. perfect; 5. mermaid; 6. furniture;
7. swerve; 8. hurricane; 9. yogurt

Page 161: Answers will vary, but should contain
the given words.

Page 162: 1. porch; 2. fork; 3. pork; 4. cork;
5. cord; 6. border; 7. torch; 8. stork;
9. scorch

Page 163: 1. dorm, form, storm, normal; 2. born,
torn, corn, worn; 3. fort, sport, short,
sort; 4. corn, sport, short, torn, storm

Page 164: 1. for, nor; 2. boar, soar, roar; 3. door,
floor; 4. four, pour; 1. roar; 2. soar;
3. door; 4. four; 5. pour; 6. floor

Page 165: 1. bore; 2. core; 3. shore; 4. more;
5. tore; 6. store; 7. score; 8. snore;
9. wore; 10. chore; 1. store; 2. core;
3. shore; 4. tore; 5. snore; 6. score

Page 166: Car: star, yard, dark, smart, farm, large;
Chair: pear, bear, pair, square, hair,
scare; **Girl:** turtle, shirt, curl, germ, dirt,
fur; **Corn:** cord, store, storm, worn,
door, pour

Page 167:

Page 168: 1. shirt; 2. nurse; 3. dart; 4. bird;
5. turtle; 6. bear; 7. door; 8. car;
9. shark; 10. corn; 11. fork; 12. girl;
13. pear; 14. star; 15. four; 16. skirt;
17. horn; 18. chair; 19. arm; 20. curl

Page 170: 1. yes; 2. no; 3. yes; 4. yes; 5. yes;
6. no; 7. no; 8. yes; 9. yes; 10. yes

Page 171: 1. phone, 1; 2. flowers, 2;
3. calendar, 3; 4. alligator, 4;
5. kitten, 2; 6. watch, 1;
7. computer, 3; 8. dinosaur, 3;
9. book, 1; 10. radio, 3; 11. finger, 2;
12. feather, 2; 13. football, 2;
14. throne, 1

Page 172: 1 syllable: rose, swing; **2 syllables:**
ladder, fifteen, castle, doughnut;
3 syllables: telephone; **4 syllables:**
California, supermarket

Page 173: 1. cap•tain; 2. cof•fee; 3. sis•ter;
4. shep•herd; 5. foun•tain; 6. pen•ny;
7. par•ty; 8. run•ner; 9. sil•ly;
10. bas•ket; 11. plas•tic; 12. swim•ming;
13. plat•ter; 14. sil•ver; 15. mis•take;
16. an•gel

Page 174: 1. be•gin; 2. ta•ble; 3. mu•sic;
4. ra•dar; 5. spi•der; 6. mi•nus;
7. ro•bot; 8. o•pen; 1. plan•et;
2. com•et; 3. mon•ey; 4. wiz•ard;
5. cab•in; 6. hon•ey; 7. jun•gle;
8. num•ber

Page 175: 1. can•dle; 2. ca•ble; 3. tur•tle;
4. this•tle; 5. cra•dle; 6. thim•ble;
7. peo•ple; 8. mar•ble; 9. bub•ble;
10. pud•dle; 11. ap•ple; 12. nee•dle;
13. ea•gle; 14. rat•tle; 15. ma•ple;
16. han•dle

Page 176: 1. cir•cle; 2. spar•kle; 3. sim•ple;
4. dou•ble; 5. tum•ble; 6. puz•zle;
7. un•cle; 8. trem•ble; 9. gen•tle;
10. wig•gle; 11. pur•ple; 12. ve•hi•cle

Page 177: 1. pi'•lot; 2. shov'•el; 3. sal'•ad;
4. ze'•bra; 5. fos'•sils; 6• ba'•con;
7. lem'•on; 8. mel'•on; 9. a'•pron

Page 178: Colored: 1. **a**way; 2. **a**bout; 3. **ball**oon;
4. so**fa**; 5. doz**en**; 6. per**son**; 7. pen**cil**;
8. pizza; 9. ap**ple**; 10. met**al**; 11. bu**tton**;
12. bub**ble**; 13. fin**al**; 14. **pa**rade

Page 179: 1. ta**ble**; 2. pen**cil**; 3. wag**on**;
4. **ball**oon; 5. pi**zza**; 6. bar**rel**;
7. ba**con**; 8. ro**bin**; 9. nick**el**

Page 180: 1. but**ton**; 2. pen**cil**; 3. sea**son**; 4. pal**ace**; 5. cac**tus**; 6. hospi**tal**; 7. per**son**; 8. ta**ble**; 9. fa**mous**

Page 181: Answers will vary, but should contain at least 6 words from the word box.

Page 182: 1. work•book, 2; 2. rab•bit, 2; 3. star, 1; 4. tel•e•phone, 3; 5. trum•pet, 2; 6. daf•fo•dil, 3; 7. poo•dle, 2; 8. po•ta•to, 3; 9. cat•er•pil•lar, 4; 10. frost, 1

Page 183: 1. dragon; 2. model; 3. again; 4. minute; 5. angel; 6. tuna; 7. panda; 8. gallop; 9. even; 10. pasta; 11. label; 12. jacket; 13. chicken; 14. lemon

Page 185: dishonest—not truthful; disarmed—having no weapon; discontinued—put an end to or stopped; disagreement—a difference of opinion; dislike—to have a feeling against something; discourage—to take away someone's hopes; disability—a loss or lack of skills; 1. disarmed; 2. discontinued; 3. disagreement; 4. dislike; 5. disability

Page 186: rewrap—to cover in something again; rewrite—to copy over again; repaint—to paint again; return—to come back again; reapply—to put something on again; rebuild—to build again; rediscover—to find again; 1. rewrap; 2. rewrite; 3. repaint; 4. return; 5. rebuild

Page 187: unwrap—to remove paper from something; unhappy—to feel sad; unknown—something that is not known; unripe—not ready to be eaten; unable—cannot do something; unkind—not a kind person; unnecessary—something that is not needed; 1. unwrap; 2. unripe; 3. unhappy; 4. unable; 5. unnecessary

Page 188: 1. **un**known; 2. **dis**agree; 3. **re**apply; 4. **dis**courage; 5. **un**sure; 6. **re**build; 7. **dis**cover; 8. **un**friendly; 9. **re**run; 10. **un**tangle; 11. **re**turn; 12. **dis**continue; Answers will vary, but should contain the given words.

Page 189: wonderful—unusually good/filled with wonder; careful—give close attention to/being cautious; thoughtful—considerate; graceful—not clumsy or awkward; fearful—afraid/not brave; helpful—useful to others; joyful—showing great happiness; 1. graceful; 2. fearful; 3. careful; 4. helpful; 5. wonderful

Page 190: thoughtless—careless/inconsiderate of others; hopeless—without hope; careless—done without paying close attention; useless—without a use; helpless—unable to help yourself; fearless—brave; harmless—not dangerous; 1. harmless; 2. thoughtless; 3. fearless; 4. useless; 5. careless

Page 191: busily—working without stopping; kindly—in a gentle or thoughtful manner; quietly—without any noise; merrily—filled with fun and laughter; quickly—in a fast way; eagerly—impatiently/with great desire; sadly—unhappily; 1. eagerly; 2. quietly; 3. quickly; 4. sadly; 5. merrily

Page 192: 1. harm**less**; 2. use**ful**; 3. quick**ly**; 4. help**less**; 5. grace**ful**; 6. soft**ly**; 7. kind**ly**; 8. hope**ful**; 9. fear**less**; 10. rest**less**; 11. happi**ly**; 12. wonder**ful**; Answers will vary, but should contain the given words.

Page 193: 1. discontinued; 2. return; 3. gracefully; 4. harmful; 5. rewrite; 6. dislikes; 7. unhappy; 8. fearless

Page 195: 1. planes; 2. dresses; 3. foxes; 4. patches; 5. stamps; 6. dishes; 7. bikes; 8. buses; 9. glasses

Basic Phonics Skills, Level D • EMC 3321 • ©2004 by Evan-Moor Corp.

Page 196: 1. berries; 2. ponies; 3. candies; 4. cherries; 5. fairies; 6. ladies; 7. monkeys; 8. boys; 9. flies; 10. daisies

Page 197: 1. puppies; 2. parties; 3. pennies; 4. Butterflies; 5. babies; 6. days; 7. flies; 8. toys; 9. cities; 10. stories

Page 198: 1. calves; 2. elves; 3. halves; 4. knives; 5. lives; 6. loaves; 7. leaves; 8. shelves; 9. wives; 10. wolves; 1. calves; 2. leaves; 3. loaves

Page 199: mouse—mice; woman—women; goose—geese; foot—feet; person—people; child—children; ox—oxen; tooth—teeth; 1. child; 2. teeth; 3. woman; 4. geese

Page 200: Add -s: pen, plane, pencil, flower, shoe; **Add -es:** kiss, pass, fox, inch, brush, dish, class; **Change y to i and add -es:** baby, berry, city, story, puppy, penny, fly; **Change f/fe to v and add -es:** leaf, knife, elf, wolf, half, calf

Page 201: 1. talking; 2. sleeping; 3. making; 4. knocking; 5. raking; 6. dancing; 7. jumping; 8. kicking; 9. shining; 10. voting

Page 202: 1. hopping; 3. skipping; 4. tapping; 6. dragging; 7. napping; 8. dripping; 1. hopping; 2. napping; 3. tapping; 4. skipping

Page 203: 1. cried, crying; 2. fried, frying; 3. dried, drying; 4. spied, spying; 5. pried, prying; 6. worried, worrying

Page 204: 1. married, marrying; 2. sprayed, spraying; 3. cried, crying; 4. carried, carrying; 5. tried, trying; 6. played, playing; 7. hurried, hurrying; 8. enjoyed, enjoying; 9. spied, spying; 10. prayed, praying; 11. relied, relying; 12. stayed, staying

Page 205: 1. quickly; 2. bravely; 3. loudly; 4. busily; 5. happily; 6. angrily

Page 206: 1. talking; 2. happily; 3. napped; 4. dancing; 5. baked; 6. practiced; 7. dragging; 8. jumping; 9. tapped; 10. making

Page 208: -ain: 1. rain; 2. train; 3. chain; **-aw:** 1. paw; 2. gnaw; 3. straw

Page 209: 1. pain, sprain; 2. rain, stain; 3. train, Spain, main; 4. strain, brain; 5. chain, drain; 6. grain, plain

Page 210: 1. straw, claw; 2. Shaw, draw; 3. paw, claws; 4. raw, slaw; 5. jaws, gnaw; 6. thaw, saw

Page 211: -are: 1. mare; 2. scare; 3. square; **-air:** 1. chair; 2. stairs; 3. repair

Page 212: 1. fare; 2. square; 3. compare, hare; 4. dare, care; 5. glare, scare, mare; 6. hare, snare

Page 213: 1. stairs; 2. air; 3. unfair, fair; 4. hair, chair; 5. pair, lair; 6. despair, repair

Page 214: -ew: 1. blew; 2. drew; 3. chew; **-ead:** 1. bread; 2. thread; 3. head

Page 215: 1. few, flew; 2. new, crew; 3. chew, stew; 4. threw, blew; 5. knew, dew; 6. brew, crew

Page 216: 1. tread; 2. lead; 3. read; 4. dread; 5. spread, bread; 6. dead, head

Page 217: -eak: 1. peak; 2. speak; 3. leak; **-eed:** 1. weed; 2. feed; 3. steed

Page 218: 1. sneak, creak; 2. squeak; 3. peak, bleak; 4. beak; 5. leak; 6. weak, speak

Page 219: 1. weeds, seeds; 2. steed, speed; 3. freed, reeds; 4. need, heed; 5. feed, seeds; 6. deed

Page 220: -oy: 1. boy; 2. toy; 3. enjoy; **-oil:** 1. boil; 2. oil; 3. soil

Page 221: 1. boy; 2. Roy, Troy; 3. soy; 4. toy, joy; 5. destroy; 6. ploy

Page 222: 1. soil; 2. spoil; 3. coil; 4. foil; 5. boil, broil; 6. oil, broil

Page 223: **-udge:** 1. fudge; 2. judge; 3. trudge;
-ight: 1. a knight in a fight; 2. a bright
light; 3. a dark night

Page 224: 1. judge; 2. grudge; 3. trudge;
4. sludge; 5. budge, nudge;
6. smudge, fudge

Page 225: 1. bright, light, night; 2. right, fight;
3. flight, right; 4. knight, fright;
5. might, light; 6. right, tight

Page 226: **-oop:** 1. hoop; 2. scoop; 3. coop; **-ook:**
1. book; 2. hook; 3. cook

Page 227: 1. snoop; 2. coop; 3. swoop, scoop;
4. droop, troops; 5. hoop; 6. sloop

Page 228: 1. crook, took; 2. hook; 3. cook, book;
4. shook; 5. look, brook; 6. nook, book

Page 229: **-ow (long o):** 1. bow; 2. row; 3. snow;
-ow: 1. cow; 2. sow; 3. plow

Page 230: 1. show, bow; 2. blow, snow; 3. know,
sow, row; 4. slow; 5. mow, stow;
6. glow

Page 231: 1. How, cow; 2. plow, now; 3. bow;
4. sow; 5. vow; 6. brow

Page 232: **-out:** 1. snout; 2. trout; 3. sprout;
-ound: 1. hound; 2. ground; 3. round

Page 233: 1. sprout; 2. trout, snout; 3. pout, trout;
4. out, shout; 5. about, Scout; 6. stout,
gout

Page 234: 1. wound, around; 2. found, hound,
mound; 3. pound, ground; 4. sound;
5. round; 6. found, ground

Page 235: **-ark:** 1. shark; 2. lark; 3. park; **-ore:**
1. store; 2. shore; 3. tore

Page 236: 1. bark; 2. park; 3. shark; 4. mark,
park; 5. spark, dark; 6. Hark, lark

Page 237: 1. snore; 2. score, more; 3. wore, sore;
4. Fore; 5. core, before; 6. more, gore,
before

                    Basic Phonics Skills, Level D • EMC 3321 • ©2004 by Evan-Moor Corp.